Other Works by Rev. Dr. Cindy Paulos

Books

Put a Little Light in Your Life, A Guide for Sending and Receiving Positive   Energy

The Travel Angel Handbook

Angel Blessings, Messages from Heaven

CD's

There is a Forever

Practicing Aloha

Angel Blessings Benefitting Hospice

Arise Above Abuse

All available at cindypaulos.com

http://www.marysmessagesoflove.com/

https://www.facebook.com/revCindyPaulos/

Mystical Mother Mary

Sacred Tools of Love

Messages, Meditations, and Prayers

Rev. Dr. Cindy Paulos, Msc.D.

Edited by Dr. Michael Likey, D.D., Ph.D., PsyTh.D., Dip.H.

ISBN: 153316231X
ISBN-13: 978-1533162311

"Whether you read this book straight through, or open it up randomly for a "message", no doubt you will be guided to a Higher Consciousness heretofore not experienced. You will be well on your way to uncovering your soul's purpose, and therefore to living a prosperous, contented life. I envy anyone who opens up this book and enters into their journey of self-discovery and growth...it's a brand-new world. Yes, thanks to Cindy and Mother Mary, a brand-new world!" ~Dr. Michael Likey, D.D., Ph.D., PsyTh.D., Dip.H.

"The Beautiful poetry that Mother Mary lovingly shares through Cindy soothes and awakens the wisdom of the heart, while offering the gift and Blessing of deep inner peace." ~Claire Papin, visionary and author of *Mary's Miracles and Messages*

"With gratitude I cherish the inspired words Cindy brings through of the Divine Mother. Her words evoke a precious understanding how Mother Mary comes to us and calls us to awaken to the Love that created us." ~Rev. Mary Omwake, Unity Minister

"Cindy Paulos has proclaimed the greatness of our most Blessed Mother Mary and of the Lord with her words of wisdom, love and peace which flows freely for all to benefit." ~Bob Miles, Television host/Author

"Cindy Paulos' voice of love and healing arises from her direct experience of the divine. Taste the ambrosia in her words." ~Arnie Kotler, Koa Books

"Cindy Paulos began her spiritual studies with me as a teenager. This started decades of her contributions of higher spiritual awareness to others. Years of devotion to higher spiritual concepts are to be found in her writings." ~Dr. Paul Leon Masters, Founder and CEO of the International Metaphysical Ministry

"I have known and worked with Cindy for decades. She is the real deal." ~Dr. Wayne Dyer, author and inspirational speaker

"Cindy Paulos is a voice for love and healing. Her dedication to service is impeccable. I love to work with Cindy, for her energy is pure and she brings such kindness to all she does. Cindy is a blessing to the world!" ~Alan Cohen, author of *A Deep Breath of Life*

Dedication

I offer this book with love to Mother Mary and to all who seek to find Her Divine blessings. It was made possible with the help of Dr. Michael Likey, Bob Miles and Rev. Mary Omwake. I dedicate it to my mother and to my daughter Heather Marie Paulos, who is the mother I was never able to be. Written in memory of my mentor, friend and step-father Dr. Paul Masters.

Contents

Forward

I find myself humbled and honored to write the forward to a book written by one of the modern mystics of our times.

I speak, of course, of the Reverend Cindy Paulos, a woman for whom I have the deepest respect and admiration for. Our paths have crossed a number of times before, as she was (and will be again) a guest on my BlogTalk Radio show; in turn, she has had me a number of times on her own show.

More than that, she is an inspiration not only for me, but for her wide audience of folks who have been blessed enough to hear her on broadcast radio as well as her numerous internet podcasts on matters spiritual, her lovely works of art on Facebook, as well as her numerous audio CD's rich with inspirational music and spoken words. She provides the once-a-week audio spoken words to her step-father's weekly "Mystical Insights" posted on the University of Metaphysics and University of Sedona's websites as well. She is beyond busy; I suspect she glides upon the gossamer wings of angels in order to do all that she does, in such smooth and concise fashion. On top of all of that, she manages to take the time to commune with the endless beauty of nature in Hawaii, where she resides; I suspect, as well, that this is the true source of her strength and inspiration. Some call the source of this inspiration God, Goddess, Mother-Father God, Source, Supreme Intelligence, I call it Love.

A brief word here about her step-father, Dr. Paul Leon Masters. During the writing of this book, Dr. Masters (as well as one of Cindy's friends and mentors, Dr. Wayne Dyer) made his transition. I cannot express in words how inspirational Dr. Masters was to myself as one of his many students of both the University of Metaphysics and the University of Sedona, both of which he founded, and both of which are also the oldest and most respected universities of their kind in the world. I earned my three doctorates through those universities, and Dr. Masters has helped shape my approach to the field of metaphysics, which in turn has endlessly helped me to assist my patients, clients, and students in their journey towards personal growth and self-empowerment. Moreover, the knowledge and information provided by Dr. Masters' universities has also shaped me in the writing of (so far to date) 15 books on metaphysics and self-help. For this, I will be eternally grateful.

All of this has worked on my consciousness in a positive way, and no doubt Cindy's, as the step-daughter of this amazing man. It is therefore indirectly through Cindy, that I can thank Dr. Masters for his wealth of Universal Consciousness imparted to us all. It is also Cindy Paulos personally, that I can thank for her wealth of knowledge, and inspirational works of art and music which still continue to motivate and to inspire me.

Moreover, it is to Cindy's latest effort, Mystical Mother Mary, that I am indebted, personally, professionally, and spiritually, for I have had the admirable task, or rather labor of love, to edit this amazing work, and in the process, it has enriched my soul. When Cindy asked me to edit this book, we both felt that it was "right", not only because I have the technical know-how to do the job, but because to quote her, "I get it". If "I get it" she means that embracing the words contained within with love, gratitude, and reverence, so be it. If she means "I get it" because I voraciously embraced and embrace every word, so be it. Simply, I relate to the contents and information, and the Mother Mary figure feels like a familiar family-member to me! I feel safe with her, because of this familiarity; I feel the same love, gratitude, and reverence as I do for Cindy. In my heart, I know this body of work will change the world as each person reads the words.

Whether you read this book straight through, or open it up randomly for a "message", no doubt you will be guided to a Higher Consciousness heretofore not experienced. You will be well on your way to uncovering your soul's purpose, and therefore to living a prosperous, contented life. I envy anyone who opens up this book and enters into their journey of self-discovery and growth...it's a brand-new world.

Yes, thanks to Cindy and Mother Mary, a brand-new world!

-**Dr. Michael H. Likey**, D.D., Ph.D., PsyTh.D., Dip.H.
April 2016, Coquitlam, Canada.

The proof is always begging to be seen by the unseen
For the unseen is always waiting to be seen.

Chapter 1

The Vision

Thou hast granted me life and mercy, and thy visitation has kept my spirit.
Job 10:12

What if the Blessed Mother Mary were to come to life right here, right now, today? What if she were to be present with you in a conversation and gave you insight on how to make your life better. What if she acted as your friend and coach and offered you ways to be more loving, compassionate, and forgiving.

Is it possible that you can embody the depth of the love Mary holds in her heart? Can you consider that Mary wants to be a part of our lives, to give us Her wisdom, kindness and strength?

Through the Mystical Path you can make that inner connection to Christ, God and Mother Mary. Christ said "The Kingdom of God is Within." That is the essence of what the Mystical path is about. Mary experienced mystical union with God. She was one of the first woman mystics. It was through her mystical union with God that the birth of Christ was born. She showed us through her example that we too can experience that inner union with God.

I have written this book to help you find a way to make that direct inner connection to the Holy Spirit. With that inner connection you can be in the presence of Mother Mary and receive her guidance. She can reach out and lift you to the higher realms of heaven. She can speak to you and heal your heart. The blessed gifts and tools she brings can transform your life. She can deliver you to Christ.

We know Christ wanted us to follow his path and he encouraged us to become like him. I believe that we can also follow the example Mary set for us. It is time for Mary's spirit to be recognized and brought into the world as never before. For the world so needs her Divine love right now. Yes, is time for Her presence to appear in us through our kindness and loving actions. At this unique time in our evolution she is more available than ever for us to reach her. She is reaching out through these words. You can find Her when you pray and meditate in so many miraculous ways.

Mary was not just a Virgin who brought us the Child of God, she also holds the Power to give us the keys to open the door of compassion and forgiveness for all beings, with the gift of mystical oneness to reach her and allow her to teach and guide us.

The Divine Feminine and Cosmic Mother holds the true image as a blueprint we can embrace that can bring us blessings beyond our comprehension. I have seen parts of that blueprint by the Grace of Mary and God and I wish to share it with you; for the time is now for us to do what we can to bring more light, love, and kindness to the world.

There is a grace of bold courage that can lead you to believe that you can call upon the Holy Mother to bring a perfect balance into your life. It can speak to you and touch your life and bring a new level of understanding that will deliver you to great joy and peace. She gives us the Power to receive the keys to open the door of compassion and forgiveness for all beings.

It matters not if you are a man or woman. The principles Mary embraced can lead anyone to be inspired to find a true connection with the Lord. This leads to a love that truly marries us to God with a sacred Love that can overcome any challenges and any fears. It leads us to understand divine principles that can change our lives for the better forever.

The mystical way of learning is to have direct contact with the source by going within. I have found that there is a way to commune with Spirit. You can learn to receive her messages. If you seek you shall find a calling to truly reach past the many distractions of the mind and life to find how this can work in the honest silence of the journey that is directed by your soul. For this journey is fueled by a calling of your heart and no one but yourself is watching.

If you do not feel worthy or if you feel too comfortable in your life you may never be driven to take that path to find out if you can have direct contact with the Divine. The mystical connection with Mother Mary takes a heartfelt commitment to the path of union with God. It is in the desiring first of the Kingdom of Heaven and to be willing to bring it to earth. It is not an easy path; it takes a lifetime, in fact. It takes a daily practice of prayer and meditation.

There is the rather long involved process of discovering a way to be able to live with what you find when you begin this journey. It is a very deep relationship that develops with the self and the higher self and the Creator. It can be all consuming and also very demanding, very addicting and very difficult. It is a path that never ever really ends. It plays out in the real world in how you live and work with what you encounter.

The proof is always begging to be seen by the unseen. For the unseen is always waiting to be seen. And then here is always this drive to be faithful to the gifts given by spirit. So forgive me if I fall short Lord. For perhaps we can only hope to try to follow the example of the teachers of the Lord.

It is easy to have an inferiority complex when you are dealing with the Master and the Queen of Heaven. Yet this is not what she would want. For she lifts up when we have fallen. We are the children of the Lord who are here to learn and grow. She is the Divine Mother and has the bigger picture that we can learn to understand and know.

I have been directed by Mary to share the keys to her Kingdom of Love. Knowing all of the challenges I'm compelled to attempt to share with you what I have learnt on this journey. Even though I feel like a student preparing to take a test to graduate. It is so easy to put off impossible tasks. And so bothersome with that little voice inside saying go ahead just do it.

Mother Mary gives us sacred tools that we can use to transform our lives. She is a kind teacher and Master who guides us with the way of love. Some of the keys she offers us that are covered in this book are Mercy, the Grace of the Holy Spirit, learning to both give and receive, love, forgiveness, overcoming being judgmental, compassion and understanding, redemption, honoring Her Angels, and the gift of prayer.

I have discovered that I am not the only one who has been called to spread her words. I have found many others who are not Catholic but have been touched by her presence and experienced her miraculous messages.

These messages are truly meditations. The book is not meant to be read all at once. It should be read a little at a time. It also does not need to be read in any particular sequence. You can open it anywhere that you feel directed to and find what you need for your spiritual inspiration.

I believe that we are at a turning point in the world and there is a need to bring our energy back into balance with the Divine. Mother Mary is calling out to her children. Listen and hear her call.

A Short Background of My Spiritual Path

I have been following the path of Mysticism for most of my life. I was around 13 when I read about many great mystics through time. And so I decided that the mystic path of direct contact would be my path.

And oh, the Glory you can find when you make that inner connection to God. Oh, the heights of the most sublime energy that can be found when you are called. That love affair with the divine is the most powerful one you can have, and the most all consuming one that you could ever imagine.

Once you have tasted the nectar of heaven it is so hard to find the earthly shadows anything but a poor reflection of the Source. Yet Christ asks us to see God in our neighbors' eyes, and to love our enemies. And life is the true test of how that hard that can be. I found that I never could fit the mold of what the average person desired from life.

It all become very clear to me one day when I had direct contact with God.

I had an experience that changed my life forever. I was 15 years old and going to Beverly Hill High School. One day I was meditating and I was lifted out of my body and mind until I was at a timeless place beyond the world. There I was consumed by a brilliant white light. It was more brilliant than a thousand suns. I experienced the power of ultimate Divine Love that opened my heart up to understand everything and nothing. There is PURE LOVE at the source of all creation. I experienced God in all of his Glory. I did not want to leave that space, I wanted to stay there and experience union with God. I felt I had a choice and I decided to return and tell others about how perfect this energy of God's love is. While you are embraced by it absolutely everything is understood. You know the Divine Plan and purpose. You also feel that everyone is choosing to be where the are in life at any given time. That their souls are playing out there roles in a destiny that will lead them to a higher path. It was an experience that changed my life forever.

Once you are in the place of divine bliss where you find absolute unconditional love it is very hard to ever want to leave. I could have stayed there but truly felt the need to serve this love by sharing it with others. Of course this is not an easy task. First, people don't want to hear or believe that you merged with God, especially at the age of 15. And so there is the cross to bear. You really can not talk about what happens in the deepest state union with God easily for it is truly beyond words.

I choose to write about my experiences through messages I receive after meditation. After about an hour of meditating I either get a phrase or seed concept that comes. Then I write in a journal what comes to me. When I was young I was extremely shy. My heart knew that I wanted to express what I was experiencing, yet I had a hard time talking about it. I knew how important it was to reach out to others, so working in radio seemed like a good way to be hidden yet heard. It is thus left to one to just live their life in a normal way with a very different perspective than others might have.

I went through many difficult situations. I experienced sexual abuse as a child and was raped at a very young age. I buried it and didn't remember what happened until, through the grace of Mother Mary, prodding me and letting me know that I was safe and protected the memories which eventually came back to me. I then was in a very violent and abusive marriage, and pregnant at the age of 17. My only solace was being able to turn within for comfort. God was always there for me, thank God!

I have followed various inner teachers in my life, and while I learnt much from studying with the masters, I have always held Christ as my true teacher. I had not in reality followed the path of any particular female Master. But of course had great respect for the two Mary's.

A few years ago I was encouraged to do a 33-day Marian retreat by my friend Bob Miles. I had no idea what a huge impact it would have on my life. I have to say not being a Catholic I had to overcome some of the language which did not feel right to me. But I did search out many other more mystical books on Mary and was guided to read about the lives of other more mystical Saints.

One in particular I felt was directed by Mary to me. She was someone who I felt a particular alignment toward. That was the enlightened Saint Hildegard of Bingen. I asked for any communication that might come as messages from Mary and Hildegard of Bingen. On a journey like this many unexpected things can happen. And they did. As a result I received a message to do what I could to help women who experienced abuse and Domestic Violence.

I also had a visitation that inspired me continue to want to share messages from Mary with a book and CD of what had come to me. I have found that I get directions in bits and pieces, and that is probably because it might tend to be overwhelming if I were to see the whole vision in detail at one time. So this book evolved piece by piece. One thing would lead to another until the pieces of the puzzle all fit in.

It is so comforting to know that the universe sends us support when needed. There have been a few people who gave me encouragement when I felt overwhelmed by the project. I have done radio shows with a dear friend Rev. Mary Omwake and we have discussed some of the subject covered here and it truly helped me to focus and receive the support needed to complete the project. Dr. Michael Likey has been such a blessing and has totally devoted himself to this book. He stepped up to the plate and gave me advice and help when I really needed it. Dyan Garris is creating heavenly music for a CD with some of these words. Bob Miles also put together a musicians to for another CD to follow. I know these people where my angels helping to guide me through this project.

In this book what I did was to get some messages, write them down, and then think of how they could be best used. I am aware that just reading words considered to be poetry is not popular to many people. That is how messages have always come to me and just recently found out that is often the way some angels communicate with people. The words are really teachings and prayers of sorts that come to me and through me.

I include some information at the beginning of each chapter on the subject matter. I also include some exercises that use light to help transform your energy field. Most of these have come to me through direction from Mary that I have used and found helpful. Some have been practices I have been doing for a while. I include meditations that you can use that make some of the information easier to use. Much of this book is designed for you to make your own connection to Mother Mary. If you can do that she will be there for you to call upon whenever you need.

I read quite a few books on Mother Mary. I found some very insightful and in some cases I would be thinking of subject and open a book to a page exactly on that topic. Some books were written hundreds of years ago by nuns who also had visitations. Many confirmations came to me while writing this book in a very interesting ways. I believe many people are responding to Mary's call. She is calling out to bring the world into balance. She is calling out to help those in need. She is calling out to ask us to save Mother Earth. She is calling out to all those who are seeking relief.

I have done much reflection on why these messages came and how they can help people who are seeking to aid the world with Her help. What I got was that on higher levels of awareness that She and the Masters hold, all of these principles expressed in the following chapters are already in place in heaven. These have been achieved after much time and work.

What we are doing here with Her help is to replicate the pre-existing way of being in these higher realms. I have been told that this is similar to what people do in yoga postures. In yoga teachers create body postures that bring about desired results that align body, mind a spirit so that one can achieve union with God. So when we practice love, compassion, kindness, forgiveness, non-judgment we are learning to exist as higher levels of consciousness do. As we learn to make them a part of our way of life we can be aligned with the higher realms of Light and have access to the wisdom and power of the Masters.

It is important to realize that it is very dangerous to give these keys to the higher realms to people who would use for their own ego and personnel gain. When you have access to the teachers and Mary you have responsibilities that come with the teachings. That is why these teachings need to be practiced daily as a way of life. It really is up to each of us to know when we are really ready to graduate and be initiated into discipleship. The rewards and gifts are many. But the challenges to live with these principles can take a lifetime of work

The energy, messages and presence I have felt from Mary are not always the same as how she has been portrayed in the past. I sense her Power and her Love. I definitely sense that she is a Master of the highest degree. That she is able to deliver us to the Christ as she delivered the Christ.

There is so much we can learn from Mother Mary that the possibilities are limitless.

I pray that these words will help you to be able to achieve an inner lasting connection to her love and help in whatever way you might need.

Mary embrace me with your love
May I see your face in others I pray,
Let your life be an example
that inspires me ever day.
Speak with whispers to my soul
Let your precious words be shown,
To place upon life's altar
So I can offer them for others to know.

Chapter 2
The Golden Orb of The World

Her ways are ways of pleasantness, and all her paths are peace.
Proverbs 3:17

Mary's Visitation and How You Can Use It In Your Life

One morning while I was doing the Marian Retreat I had a vision of Mary come to me. I had said my prayers and called upon her to be with me. I went into a deep meditation and sensed a Divine presence with me. There was a definite shift in energy. I sensed her before I saw her. The presence she carried and carries was alive in Spirit. I felt a movement in the air, a slight breeze which still often surrounds me when I call upon her. She came in a shimmering energy of Higher Light.

When I saw her she was before me wearing a beautiful deep royal blue robe. I sensed it was a shroud of mercy and protection. She had a crown of radiant living stars that shone around her head. They sparkled and were more brilliant than any diamond I had ever seen. In fact, they were alive and in tune with her divine energy and with her smiling face. She was indeed a loving presence that was so full of understanding and great compassion. It felt as if she knew everything about me, all that had happened to me, and all that has yet to happen.

She reached out her hand and gave me a glimmering golden globe and I reached out to receive this blessed gift. I felt transformed and I could feel the powerful energy of the globe. I knew it represented the world. I should explain that it is a pure golden globe in her hands, however, when it is handed over, (specifically to myself) it is not visible yet it can be felt as a radiant energy field. I felt it had a weight even though it could not be seen.

Many statues and paintings have the same image of Mary wearing a blue robe a with a crown of stars. Not all had the golden globe, so I "Googled" that and came up with an image similar to what Saint Catherine Laboure saw, which inspired her to create a Miraculous medal in 1830. This Golden Globe symbolized the world and the responsibility to hold the light of this orb as a symbol of saying prayers for the world.

I realized we can symbolically wear Mary's Robe of mercy and protection. We can symbolically bring the crown of stars down from heaven to wear over our head. We can symbolically reach out and take the Golden Globe offered to all who will take it. We each can do this and make the world a better place for it.

Mary has great concern the what is happening on Mother Earth and that includes the well being of the planet and the need for the world to bring awareness to the need for more peace and love.

I know we all know the world needs more love, however, with Mary I feel as if I know that she really experiences all of the suffering going on in the world firsthand. When you sense this in her you cannot but want to help.

Mary asked me to share her messages. She feels that it is time for all the people in the world to know what she can offer. She clearly wants people to know she is there for EVERYONE in the world. She is not just for Catholics. Everyone can benefit from her kind and loving support. She makes us want to be a better person. She conveys Her need to help all the suffering people on this planet and she needs us to help.

So many people do not understand that Mary is for everyone. It is strange because I have had this point reinforced very clearly many times since her visit. Many times I have mentioned to others that I am working on a book about Mother Mary; the response is often similar to, "The Catholic Mary?", or "Are you Catholic." I am not Catholic and I do want to say the Catholics certainly knew what they were doing when they started honoring her so long ago. I have no wish to offend the Catholics or any religion.

I also have found it interesting that many who meditate and love angels feel no connection to Mother Mary. I was talking to a friend who is putting on an Angel Summit. I told her I was working on a book about Mother Mary, and once again I heard, "Oh, the Catholic Mary?" It was not until I reminded her that Mary is the Queen of Angels that she began to think of her in terms of angels. Angels have gained great popularity worldwide, yet people do not consider Mary as the Queen of Angels.

The world is awakening to a new level of awareness and it is time for

Mother Mary and her gifts to be offered to ALL who need help. Am I an expert on Her? No, by no means. I questioned myself and her many times about whether I would be taken seriously, or even believed at all.

I realize that I may offend some Catholics and some Christians, and that many in the New Age community will not understand. So I am doing this on my faith in Her and God. It is not a blind faith, it is a faith that has been affirmed in my life, time and again over dozens of year; I must do what I feel guided to by my heart, and as a servant of God.

Every time I questioned myself whether I should do this book or not, I went into meditation and prayer to get an answer. Every time I asked I received the message "Do it, I'll be there to guide you. It is time to reach out to more people about a way to make a direct connection to God and Christ through me. It is time to balance the world's energy with the power of Love."

I have been writing messages down after daily meditation and prayer for over 50 years. I have been a vegetarian since I was 15, and now I'm mostly Vegan. I still don't feel worthy to even attempt to honor Her correctly, for it is so hard to convey in words all that she is and all She can do. I know it's more than submitting a resume to apply for a job, in order to write her messages, for these gifts, these abilities are not developed through college degrees or scholastic credits, nor is it a regular job or position: Mary is looking for a heartfelt commitment, a commitment that is not a job, but a lifestyle and passion! She also wants me to reach out to others to connect with her as well. So who am I to doubt her? Though it still feels like I have to explain myself about how I've come to writing a book on Mother Mary, all that I can say is that I'm still getting inner urgings from her each day to do this.

I feel so humble and touched by her loving guidance and kindness that I agreed to do what I could do to write down her messages and share them. I ask for your patience and forgiveness if I fall short or offend in any way. For I am but a pilgrim and I have been on this path for a very long time. I still have so much to learn, yet I am not sure how much longer I have here. I will share all I can with a Prayer to the Mother for her loving compassion and guidance. As Teilhard de Chardin said,

"Our Duty, as men and women, is to proceed as if our ability did not exist. We are collaborators in Creation."

I wrote a prayer of commitment to Mother Mary when I finished my Marian retreat. I picked one prayer they had that I felt aligned with, and then as guided wrote one of mine which is read by me every day.

Beloved Mary, Queen of Angels Prayer

Beloved Mary Queen of Angels
You who hold open heavens space,
Help me to have compassion
And forgiveness to heal the past,
And bring me to your holy Grace.

Mary Holy Mother, I call upon your energy
I ask you bring the Holy Spirit
To be alive inside of me.

Let me share the breath of your being
To live within the heart of God's great love,
I dedicate my path to the purpose
That you have shown for me to know.

With your tender understanding
You open up the door
To the chosen one
And deliver me to the Lord.

Let me be anointed
By the holy waters from the source,
Let it quench my thirst for the beloved One
So I may serve as you would on Earth.

Be my guide and teacher
Let me honor the Light of your Golden Orb,
For the world's in needs of your mercy
Let my love help to bring it forth.

Bring the crown of stars you wear
Down to circle me,
Let me wear you're holy robe
So I can be surrounded with protection
To fulfill my destiny.

Let me breathe that holy spirit
Of the living light,
So I may be with God in the service

As a disciple in my life.

Allow the grace of your being
To transform my old mistaken ways,
Let your inspiration guide me to you
When I'm lost and know not what to do.

Holy Mother full of Grace
Remove the binds of egos ties,
Unchain the limitations
And Free me from the lies.

Embrace me with your love
May I see your face in others I pray,
Let your life be an example
That inspires me ever day.

Speak with whispers to my soul
Let your precious words be shown,
To place upon life's altar
So I can offer them for others to know.

Thank you Holy Mother
For your patience and your grace,
Thank you Holy Spirit
For your presence that leads the way
And guides me with patience and understanding every day.

The Mystical Light of the Mother

Mystical light of the Mother,
Holy Spirit so Divine,
Touch my inner heart
And join your life with mine.

May I be an instrument
Of your amazing Grace,
May your words speak through me
To share loving embrace.

Let me breathe your presence
Into my very soul,

Let me hold the chalice
From which the fountain of heaven flows.

Anoints us with the nectar of manna,
With the smile that truly shows,
The love that lives eternally
And through God's creation unfolds.

The blessings of the universe
Shine throughout all time,
With your compassion that guides
A way to forgive and find a peace divine.

Mystical Mother Mary
I offer my service to you,
May the blessings you bring
Help free those who are suffering.

May your loving kindness
Bring the darkness to light,
To allow the wonder of your miracles
Bring forth more love to our lives.

I not only have gotten wonderful words from Mary but also was given certain Light exercises and visualizations to activate a higher energy alignment to bring in her presence. I was told that we can do an exercise to recreate this visitation.

I include in this section a recreation of what I experienced as visualizations and Light exercises given by Mary to me to share with you. The first is a visualization of receiving the Golden Orb. The next is a visualization of wearing a Robe of Protection. There is also a Crown of Stars exercise.

First I'll share the Golden Orb Exercise. I now start each morning and evening mediation with this exercise.

It seems to me that the act or reaching out to her activates her ability to give. When you do this exercise wait until you feel the energy field of the Golden Orb in your hand.

The Golden Orb Exercise

Breathe in the light of Father-Mother God see that light come from the heavens down through you,
Breathe in the light of Father-Mother God.

God's light from heaven's Highest Realms flows through your chakras, the crown on your head to your heart, and then breathe out the love you receive from your heart to Mother Mary.

Do this again three times.

Receive the blessings of the presence of Mother Mary and visualize her in front of you. Feel the Presence be in her Divine Presence.

Breathe in the presence of Mother Mary and send love from your heart to her heart.

And see it this love spiraling back to you.

She holds a radiant Golden Orb in her hands.

Now hold out your right hand to receive the Golden Orb that she has. Keep your palm up and receive the Golden Orb into your hand.

Feel the warmth of life in this Golden Orb; see the power and energy and love from this Golden Orb, then let yourself actually visualize this Golden Orb as the world, surrounded with the golden light.

Feel the blessing of this divine gift.

Feel love, and the gift of this Golden Orb in your hand until you actually feel your hand palm vibrating with energy of love, and that love is a gift of the Golden Orb.

Now place your hand over your heart and let the love of this Golden Orb spiral its energy deep into your heart of hearts.

Breathe in this love; let the light of this Golden Orb completely fill your entire being with love; breathe in the love. Receive the love.

Let the love, love, love clear any blocks or fears.

Let it heal your heart.

Now take your right hand and extend it back out to mother Mary;
See Mother Mary who is holding the world in her hands,
And let your love spiral back out to her and the world that she holds.
See her receiving the love as the world is vibrating with a golden light
Send this love and light for seven breaths, out to the world saying "Love, love, love", to the world and circle it with the love in her hands.

Now thank the Holy Mother for her blessings of the Golden Orb that she holds in her hands.

Send her your love and gratitude for the great light, for the blessings that She has given to you in the world.

Mary's mission is to help the world and Mother Earth; if we wish to help as well, we can use the Golden Orb to learn how to send Divine love

30

to the World.

Mother Earth is in need of our love and we can visualize the Orb as the world in our hands.

When we hold the Golden Orb we can send the energy of Love and Light to it as if it was the world in our hands. We can say prayers for peace for the world.

Below are a few to use. After reading some prayers for peace send the world the blessings of Peace. See the Dove of Peace come and shed a light of Peace to the planet.

Visualize a world understanding that we all are one in Spirit. And let the Golden orb shine with a Holy light of Peace.

Shine the world with a balancing energy for the healing for the planet.

A Prayer for Mother Earth

Oh Great Spirit, we send our light and love for the healing of planet Earth and to the existence of the plant, animal and mineral kingdoms, and to all beings incarnate and disincarnate. May we help to balance, restore, and heal the polarities, rhythms, and cycles of natural forces. May peace and good will guide those who work together to serve the planet so God's Plan may be fulfilled for the highest good of all.

The Soul of Mother Earth

Honor the soul of the Mother Earth,
For she holds the force of Creation
That is present in the life force
That is born of such a fiery birth.

The power of the elements
Which she does hold,
The presence of spirit and matter
Merged with magic for all to behold,
With the sacred beauty so Divine
Alive in the power of Creations Mind.

Given to us as our home away from home
The place we live as guardians,
That we care for and grow
And receive her gifts with humility
And respect for our sacred home.

With the commitment to care for her
And honor and cherish and share,
All that we have in our brief time here
So we can restore the balance and polarities.

This world is in such need
It's up to us find a way to heal
The damage that's been done,
And help to be able to realize
That we are all one.

We are here for just a short while on Mother Earth
Who we should cherish and love
And help bring forth
What she needs to receive
With our dedication and energy.

The fire, the air, the water, the earth,
Needs be restored to balance
As we recognize the perfection
And beauty of the face of Creation's Face,
Reflected so perfectly in this sacred place.

We are alive and we should be
Able to dedicate our gratitude each day,
By honoring Her and helping to be
The solution for saving Her
And protecting this precious place called Mother Earth.

Open the Door

Open the door to the heart of all life
There you'll find the source of love,
Go into brilliance of God's Divine Light
And let it feed your very soul.

Light of all lights shine upon us,
Love of the great One be shown,
Source and Creator bless our lives
To be an instrument of Your Love.

Let us drink from the nectar

Of the sacred cup,
Let us be baptized by the waters
That Your Divine Presence offers.

Right here in this very moment
In this Eternal Now,
Let us honor Your Presence
And share the blessings You allow.

Heartbeat of the our Maker
That created this our life,
Whose Light shines through the firmaments
And feeds the sunlight upon the earth.

Let us be in tune with Your energy
And the Power that You give,
To let us be able to be receivers
So we can better serve Your Gifts.

Open up the doorway
To the Higher Realms,
So we can be a bridge from earth
To heaven, our eternal home.

Thank you Holy Mother
For the grace that you do bring,
Thank-you for delivering us
To the throne of the King of Kings.

The Holy Dove of Peace

From the Holy Dove of Peace
Comes a feather that falls,
To take and hold on to
And carry to the place of hope for all.

And the still point that is the resource
Of all light and love,
Comes the source of understanding
From where this peace began.

Accept there is this world of strife,

Accept that we together we can change,
To release the anger and the hatred
And see the other side as one again.

For love has always been stronger by far
Than the darkness of illusion,
That chains us and that bar
The truth that will one day win in the end.

And in time we will find forgiveness,
Hold the power and the secret key,
And it will open up the heart
To finding the way to live in peace.

It is possible to find that place within
Where we can discover the power of the way,
To be still and be at peace
And from that point be still and stay.

And the blessings of each finding
A way to find the holy dove,
And hold the feather of hope
And let the world healing begin.

The Courage to Choose Peace

Where do you find the courage
To let all the hate and resentment go?
To get past the anger and hatred,
You must view life from a point in your soul.

There past the limitations of the little mind
There is place of forgiveness you find,
And a Peace that is a state you can live with,
It is there and dwells so deep inside.

Find that place of peace within you,
Find the power it holds,
For peace is the true answer
That holds the keys for the world to know.

Past the veils of darkness and illusions

That tear the world apart,
Past that downward spiral you can choose
The path for healing to start.

Find the courage to make a difference,
Become a part of the peacemakers who pray.
To truly make the changes needed
To create a better world that together we can make,
Become part of the millions
Who wish to find that place of peace.

Blue

Heavenly Blue of the Holy Mother
Is the light that holds heavens floor,
Translucent is the vision
From the realms the angels adore.

A blue that holds the Mother's robe
And the stars that as a crown abide,
A circle of 12 that shine so Bright
Crown her head with a brilliance where heaven resides.

Bring that radiant light forth,
Bring it to that inner space,
As a circle that can spiral forth
As a ray to heal and bring you such amazing grace.

Receive the sacred blessings
That the Queen of Angels Brings,
Commit your self to serve the one
That the Holy Mother sees.

Make a vow to serve with love
And dedicate yourself to be,
One who works to help the world
To live the way of Peace.

Heavenly Blue Light,
Let your blessings be
Able to bring the grace of God

Here to us to help us heal.

Deliver to us your glory,
Deliver us to your grace;
Let the heavenly blue shine forth
The Crown of Stars to shine
Throughout all time and space.

Let Your Light Be Seen

Let your light be seen,
Let your truths be told,
Let your life be a reflection
Of the insights you've been shown.

Say "yes" to the power,
Do not be afraid;
To become the embodiment
Of Gods Love guiding your way.

Let the blessings be given
To those who do seek,
To further the work
Of the Creator's Blessings to see.

That we are one in our purpose,
We are united in our hearts,
To help the Mother and the Lord
We must serve and do our part.

So celebrate the manifestation
Of the work that comes to be,
The new way of bringing
A balance to life and a Higher Reality.

We all are imperfect,
We're all here to learn,
We all make mistakes
And yet we still affirm.

To believe it is possible
To live out the plan,
To let our souls guide us
For the betterment of our fellow humans.

And miracles will be sown,
And the light it will grow,
And in time you will find
God's gifts will enlighten.

And the light will be seen,
And the love will then lead,
The path of the soul
Will become clear and be known.

Let your mercy lift the veil
And bring the power to prevail,
With the breath of your pure space
You find blessings of love's way.
Mercy is being able to see the whole of everything
And still accept and love, all the good, all the bad,
All the dark and light that life will bring.

Chapter 3

The Robe of Protection and the Crown of Stars

I will greatly rejoice in the LORD, my soul shall be joyful in my God; for he
has clothed me with the garments of salvation, he has covered me with the
robe of righteousness, as a bridegroom decks himself with ornaments, and
as a bride adorns herself with her jewels.

-Isaiah 61:10

Mother Mary's Holy Robe has special powers.
I was told that we can visualize that robe of protection around us to shield
us from negative energy.
The robe has special qualities of mercy and protection. In various painting
it can be seen in different colors. When I saw Her, I saw her with a
beautiful robe of blue. Here are a couple of messages I received about the
Robe of Protection:

We can each wear a Robe of Protection and Mercy, it gives. You can
also use this as an exercise to do when you go into meditation or before you
go to sleep at night.

People have been using white light for protection for years, but this is a
more personal way to use light to protect you to be aligned with your own
soul energy.

If you wish to use this as a visualization you can go into a state of quiet relaxation, light a candle, and then take a few deep breaths. Call upon the presence of Mother Mary to be with you. Read one or more of the following messages from Mary. Then see your self being dressed by the angels in a heavenly Robe of Protection and Mercy. See the very threads of your soul's light weaving the radiant colors of your robe of protection. It is a beautiful shimmering robe of etheric light that you can wear. It is invisible to others, but as visible as your aura is in a high vibrational field.

It is the Robe of the disciple that holds your protection and commitment to the path you follow that holds your soul's purpose in life.

Such magnificent robe of protection
The blessed Mother wears,
Placed upon her shoulders by her son
When she took her place on heaven's throne.

And we can wear a heavenly robe
To protect us on the path we go,
It carries the energy of the soul
With radiant colors of the rainbow.

It can bring us mercy so we can be
Able to live with grace and be free,
From negative forces and energy
That would block our true destiny.

So wear the robe of mercy
Wear the robe of light,
Let it bring you the protection
And mercy in your life.

For the path is long
And we will be tested,
So we need to be strong
As we follow the Christ's Great light.

We can wear the disciples robe
Made from the pure energy of our soul,
To protect us with love and divine mercy
To help us fulfill our destiny.

The Robe of Light

The Angels of the Lord came to me,
And lifted me to a place of radiant light,
And they surrounded me with love
As I was embraced with gifts of their delight.

They offered me a cloak to wear,
For my protection while I am here.
It was made of precious energies
And lit with jewel-like colors of radiant light.
There was a shining of this robe
That was of precious gold so bright.

It was placed upon my shoulders,
And I felt a transformation come to me,
And a bringing of new power
With highest blessings I gladly received.

I was told it was to wear for protection,
So I could be healed from the negative energy
That I had absorbed while I was here.
This cloak would help restore me 'til all was right.

And my soul was alive in it,
For the robe was a gift of love
From the angels and the Masters,
Who do the work of God for me and you.

On this journey that we started so very long ago,
There comes a time on the path
When we are given the help we need to renew.
You know that when you ask for help, it will come to you.

It's been a long, long road,
And the end is not yet in sight,
And sometimes we need to stop and rest,
And reflect on all that's needed to get us through the night.

I behold the blessings given to us,
And feel great gratitude to wear
The robe of the pilgrim,
To feel these gifts of God's love and light

That come when needed to me and you.

Wearing the Robe

Mary wore a Robe of Blue
As we as disciples can do,
It is a holy energy
An etheric protective quality.

As a servant of her great love
The one who delivers us to grace,
We can live a better life
To help overcome our fellow humans plight.

Mary wore a robe of Blue
As we her servants can do,
For we are in tune with her energy
And embrace the truth to set us free.

Mary wore a robe of Blue
It is a protective cloak divine,
That dresses her with the beauty
Given by God and it holds a blessing for mankind.

And if we feel worthy
We certainly can accept the plan,
To live to help in any way we can
And to serve our fellow humans.

We can be disciples of the Lord,
We can devote our hearts to love,
We can have compassion and grace
And see God in the world.

And see all of the children of God
Who are in such need of Love,
And can be saved by the spirit
By the holy ones.

And so we learn to serve
With Mary's compassion and Grace,

And we can wear the robe of Mary
And help the human race.

Mary's Cloak of Grace

A cloak of grace is offered
As creations robe from this majestic cloud,
Of blue, purple and golden rays
That drapes my soul with the Mothers Love.

And I fall upon my knees and pray
And I reach deep into my heart,
And surrender to the love that can redeem us
And help us to find a new way.

And we breathe in this gift
Of which the song of heaven sings,
And we wish to merge with it
And become that spirit we find in everything.

We try to understand the miracles
That somehow Her grace brings,
And when we finally can observe it
There is so much mercy that we really need.

To release our judgments
And all that might tangle up our mind,
'Til we find we need God's mercy and forgiveness
To know there is a higher path to find.

For with time we learn and grow
And that we always have that choice to be,
With the living grace of God and the Blessed Mother
And the mercy that she brings with such great Blessings.

The Robe of Mary's Love

Let me wrap around me the robe of Mary's pure love
I've seen that robe the angels wear,
And in those folds I find the strength
Of such beauty and divine protection there.

Let my mind encompass
The radiance of the diamond's light,
That's shining forth in the Creator's Source
Of the Christ consciousness so bright.

Let my heartbeat carry the sound
Of God's breath of spirit,
And the universal pulse of all life.

And let the Mother guide me
As on this path I walk,
To reach that place of peace
So I may help in any way I might.

And there is a holy star to guide me
From the darkness to the dawn,
I see it shining forth early each morning
On this journey that I'm on.

May we see clearly from that light
To our souls so we may know,
We are all joined in this circle of life
As on the road we go.

And the spirit of God's love reveals itself
As we play our different roles,
And we learn to wear that robe of love
And uncover what is hidden deep in our soul.

How do your dress the love She imparts
The Father, the Mother, and the Son,
That live in this energy we
Are, if we stand in the center of the love,
That has been alive through eternity

And if you look deep within you will be able to feel
And the heartbeat of the world that lives in you and me,
All wrapped in the robes of the blessings of life
And the energy of the Mother's love.

We can wear the Robe of Mary, we can bring the crown of stars down from heaven to wear over our head. We can reach out and take the Golden

Globe offered to all who will take it.

We can say prayers for Peace for the world. We can show Mercy. We can care for Mother earth and pray for the balancing of energies to bring the planet back into balance.

Mercy

The Robe can provide Comfort and Mercy as well, so if your feeling in need of comfort you can say one of the following messages.

Mary is often called upon when there is a crises in someone's life. Many pray to her for a miracle or Mercy when they are feeling overwhelmed by Life.

Mercy is a blessings that is given by God if it is His Will for the highest good. We often can't even begin to know what the highest good might be for us. So we must trust in God to do what if for the best in the overall scheme of the greater good for all involved.

Here are a few prayers and messages that can be used for Comfort and Mercy.

Comfort Me Mary

Comfort me Mary
Feed this hungry soul,
Let me retreat to your sacred place
And find the windflower that speaks
Secrets in silence of the unknown.

Come and sing
Bring forth praises of exultation bring
Your joy to envelop
All my ancient dreams.

Come now and let me understand
How to serve your love with compassion,
Forever held in your hands
For all our fellow man.

Comfort me with the peace
That is there when I retreat,

To your heart held space
That holds such divine grace.

And let your mercy lift the veil
And bring the power to prevail,
With the breath of your pure space
You find blessings of love's way.

Mercy is being able to see the whole of everything
And still accept and love, all the good, all the bad,
All the dark and light
That life will bring.

Mercy Is

Mercy is the Breath of God's Spirit
The taking in and the letting go,
The birthing, the dying,
The power and strength to not know.

Mercy is
Asking and giving compassion
Asking for the strength to forgive,
And to be forgiven
To survive and thrive.

Mercy is
A Prayer, a meditation,
A hope, and the acceptance,
To be able to understand
When there are no clues.

Mercy is Alive
In the miracle of a second chance,
And to awaken to a brand new day
Without stopping or thinking,
Just partaking in the Divine Dance.

Mercy is
The light at the end of the Tunnel
To open the heart and smile again,

This amazing Grace
Given by Mary's Divine blessing,
A gift to be redeemed and live again.

Mary We Ask For Mercy

Mary we ask for Mercy
From the worries of the world,
While we're on this journey
We'll find its hard to not feel the pain.

We see so much suffering
We can't help to want to complain,
But then the chance of Holy Grace
Comes and guides us to a higher place.

And we ask for mercy
So we can let God's work be done,
First a little mercy
So we can know your there.

And if we show some kindness
And if we really care,
It may be a good place
To let compassion appear.

May we find that Mercy
And forgiveness for others who are lost,
In darkness and illusion
With the drive of ego's cause.

We ask for a little Mercy
We are silent and we pray,
For a second chance
To let love guide the way.

We thank you Mother Mary
We thank the lord above,
We are blessed by the holy spirit
And the gift of the divine dove.

Thank you for the grace,
Thank you for the blessings
Of the beauty of this place,
Thank you for the key
That comes with this Mercy that frees.

And If You Feel Weary

And Mary said to me,
If you feel weary
Please call on me
And allow yourself to be

Blessed with my Presence
And the Holy Spirit to guide you, please,
I am here with you always
If you just believe.

I am here in your times of trial,
I am here in the darkness
When you're lost and can't find
A way to find peace of mind,
And when you are lost you can be found.
There is a Light that will guide you on
From the shadows that block your way,
I am here to see you through to a brighter day.

And if you feel weary,
Please call on me
And allow yourself to be
Blessed with My Energy.

My Spirit will guide you
And you'll find relief,
If you can just believe
I am here for you when you're in need.

We can wear the Robe of Mary, we can bring the Crown of Stars down from heaven to wear over our head. We can use these messages and words to inspire us and to reach out to Mother Mary.

There are many who have been touched by her Mercy, Forgiveness,

Strength and Grace. We can reach out and take the Golden Globe, offered to all who will take it. We can be energized and protected by the robe we wear.

For we are agents of God. When we take on the role of sharing Peace, Love, and Mercy

We need to be free of taking on the burdens of suffering many go through.

We certainly can be compassionate and we can pray and send out light and love.

But it is God's Will and Mary's work to provide miracles and blessings.

We can be messengers and agents for goodwill and peace. That is how God and Mary work through us. However, it is not us, but God and Mary working through us to do the work at hand.

We are blessed to wear the Robe of Protection that helps us and shields us in ways we may never even be aware of.

So wear the Robe of Protection and Mercy and work with God and Mother Mary as a disciple of their love. Knowing that as Christ reminded us it is not us but the Father that doeth the work.

Give great thanks for being able to be an instrument for their light and love

Pick the Golden flower and Inhale the fragrance so divine,
Let the wind speak Her name
And allow it to open your heart and claim.
The gift of love is given with an open heart,
an open mind and a circle with no beginning or end

The Mother is a flower, a pure reflection
of Gods creation and perfection
A flower that baths in the Light of the Son
That penetrates through to the source of the One.

Chapter 4
She Wears a Crown of Stars

And a great sign appeared in heaven: a woman clothed with the sun, with
the moon under her feet, and on her head a crown of twelve stars.
Revelation 12:1

The Crown of Stars

When I had the vision of Mary, one of the most striking things I saw was
the Crown of Stars she wore on her head.

Almost every statue and painting of Mary show her with a Crown of
Stars. However, what was so striking was the fact that she had real living
stars around her head. Stars that were brilliant beyond description. It was as
if stars from the cosmos had come down right there on her head.

Each star had a different energy field and sparkled with shades of
different colors.

I felt as if each star was a connection to the universe and provided a
cosmic link.

Imagine if you saw a living link on your computer screen and if you
clicked it, it would take you right to where you wished to go, literally
beaming you up to heaven and beyond.

That was the power of the Crown of Stars.

I was given an exercise to share to do to connect you to the Crown of
Stars and to use them to clear any negative energy from your aura. I have
two light exercise and some of the messages I received about the Crown of

Stars.

Crown of Stars Exercise

Focus on the highest realms of heaven,
To the throne of the Holy Mother's space.
See that you are being sent a crown of stars,
    It is spiraling down from heaven
    In circles of Gold and Blue light,
    It comes down and circles around your crown chakra.

It now continues to circle downwards around the outside of your body,
Clearing away any negative energy that might be in your aura
'Till it reaches down to the ground around you.
Repeat the exercise three times.
Here are a few messages about the connection to the Cosmic Mother.

The Light of Her Stars

What spark could light that star
That shines from so far?
With her blessings it can reach me here,
To speaks a universal language when it appears.

And what creates those clouds across the sky
That come like those thoughts that cross my mind?
And they can hide the light of those billions of stars
And they can distract my presence of a soul to find.

So I burn away the clouds with a breath
That sweeps away the thoughts in my mind,
And reach and draw back the cover
That hides this grace of such love to find.

And I open up my heart and ask to receive
The love that is the perfect fire
Of Mary's amazing energy,
And the sacred teachings we can receive.

And here we all are
In this miraculous space and time,

With her stars dancing in the crown of mystic fire
And the sparks that catch me to remind.

We are all one in this light of creation
Made with the source that brought this amazing energy,
So we can look up and wish upon those stars
And see stars that Mary wears.

We can bring them down to earth
And let their power do their work,
The gift of the Crowns pure energy.

What spark could light that star
That shines from so far?
With her blessings it can reach me here
To speak a universal language when it appears.

And what creates those clouds across the sky
That come like those thoughts that cross my mind?
And they can hide the light of those billions of stars
And they can distract my presence of a soul to find.

So I burn away the clouds with a breath
That sweeps away the thoughts in my mind,
And a reach and draw back the cover
That hides this grace of such love to find.

And I open up my heart and ask to receive
The love that is the perfect fire
Of Mary's amazing energy,
And the sacred teachings we can receive.

And here we all are
In this miraculous time and space,
With her stars dancing in the crown of mystic fire embrace
And the sparks that catch me with her grace.

We are all one in this light of creation
Made with the source that brought this amazing energy,
So we can look up and wish upon those stars
And see stars that Mary wears.

We can bring them down to earth

And let their power do their work,
The gift of the Crowns pure energy.

Cosmic Stardust

We are the Cosmic stardust
From the energy of the one,
We are merged with dark and Light
The day and night of the wheel of love.

And from the one who plants the seeds
That can grow and bloom with each birth,
There is a little magic that happens
That brings Her heaven here to Earth.

And we can breathe the fragrance
Of a flower from the Light,
And we can be lifted to heaven
And remember what matters and what is right.

In every seed of Light
There is a power that can grow,
To help those who are in need
To understand so they can know.

We are the stewards of the garden
And we understand the plan,
And care for the ones who grow the seeds
From heaven to the garden to feed the souls of man.

We are the gardeners of the cosmic field
Of energy that we were given to know,
We are the stewards of heaven on earth
And we can share the harvest from our souls.

And the blessings that come from the planting
Of the seeds of the light of our souls,
Can feed the hungry masses
Who are waiting for this pure love on Mother Earth to grow.

The Stars

Through the swirling stars
That dance like Van Gogh's dreams,
There is a certain strange mystery
That entices me to want to still believe.

That there is this infinite gift of time and space
Which we can use to create and be,
The magicians who ask to receive
And absorb and the Spirit we breathe.

And this precious soul that is there
Through all of our many lives,
As we are drawn between dark and light
And this strange experience of life.

And Cosmic Mother brings this light forth
And carries the Spirit so Divine,
With this exquisite beauty that is so hard to define
Which could be why everyday I always try and try.

And this life that is given to us
To choose how we experience what we want to be,
All just part of the Mystic dance as we fly
With the invisible partner we can't quite reach.

Yet if we spin and swirl like a dervish
Through this universal dream,
And surrender to the divine mystery
One day her stars will sing.

And we might be blessed to finally hear
That elusive heavenly music of the spheres,
And we can leave the dream behind
And awaken to our true self that is the dreamer of the dream.

Fragrance of the Stars

Sweet fragrance of the stars,
The blossom of light is growing
In the garden of delight
That touches deep within my soul.

Pick the Golden flower
Inhale the fragrance so divine,
Let the wind speak Her name in silence
And allow it to open your heart and claim.

The gift of love is given with
An open heart, an open mind
And a circle with no beginning or end
Which to share this energy with a friend.

So the Mother is a flower, a pure reflection
Of God's creation and perfection,
And as the flower baths in the sun
And feels the light penetrate through to core.

So that the color of the flower
Is radiating the very light of the sun,
So you can shine forth your beauty
And become the flower of the Son.

So are you a flower of God
Blossoming in the garden,
Do not question how a flower grows
But feel the holy light of Love.

Feel the love the Creator
Of this wondrous garden where you dwell,
By being the flower of God
You will find you need to be nourished
In the world where you have chosen to grow.

The Star that Guides You Through

The seeds of your true purpose
Are alive within your soul,
You have the fire of Spirit
To burn away the illusions
So you can let go,
And let God be in Control.

If you can Believe
You will in time be shown,
How to plant the seeds of love
And find a way to let it grow.

Into a blossom with the Divine Fragrance
That carries the heavenly beauty of life,
A rose of Mary's making
A star that shines through the night.

You can hold a torch that lights
The beacon in your soul,
A star to lead through the darkest night
And lead you on the way to go.

The seeds of your true Purpose
The power to see it through,
The grace of understanding
Can be born again in you.

Let the fire burn oh so bright
Let the soul be seen,
Be true to what you came here for
And in time the truth will be seen.

Become the living light
And let the Holy Mothers words reveal,
The grace of the Masters work
And the divine blessings it will bring.

You Are a Star of Light and Love Exercise

Breath in deep the Love of God into your heart.
Release all thoughts and concerns.
 Breath in the pure of love of Mother Mary into your heart.
 Now if you are sitting, imagine a 5 pointed star
 You are going to embody this star
 See points of the radiant light of a star on either shoulder
 And a line of light connect down at the base of your spine
 See a star of light there at the base of your spine.
 So that a downward triangle is being formed
 Now see both of your hip bones as points of stars light going to the top
of your head and Meeting in a triangle
 You know have a triangle of light going down from your shoulder to the
base of your spine
 And one triangle of flight going from your hips to the point on the top
of your heard.
 This is forming a 6 pointed star.
 Now see a star of light in a upward facing triangle in the heart center.
 Let this triangle spin like a prayer wheel clockwise round in circles.
 It clears away any ancient wounds and fills the body with light and love
 You have become a star of light and love.

There are these Prayers sent by Heaven
And the angels who watch over you,
With light that will heal
And give you the strength you need to renew.

The Prayers sent by Heaven
Are there to receive,
With Blessings so true
If you can just be open and believe.

Chapter 5

Communicating with Mother Mary

Blessed are they that hear the word of God and keep it
(Luke 11:28)

I love the word "Communicate". It's wonderful to commune with others by talking and listening. When we communicate with Spirit there is a true communing that happens. There is an exchange of energy and we can truly be transformed by these holy communications.

As I reflect on the gifts given to me by Mary that can benefit others, I feel that the blessing of being able to communicate and talk to Mary and receive her messages could be the greatest gift.

It is very simple, but it takes Faith and commitment to make it possible.

To communicate with the Presence of Mary, I have a simple and time-tried process that I practice and you can as well.

First go to a quiet place to meditate.

Light a candle. Do some deep clearing breaths. Breathe in the Light of God, and release any thoughts or concerns. Breath in Peace, breath out tension. Breath in Love and let go of any fear.

Once you open up a method to connect with Mother Mary you will find it gets much easier reaching her the more time goes by. In time you will feel as if she were always right there by your side.

It can be helpful to say a few prayers, and set your intention, and then to be open to spirit. I have included prayers that you can use if you choose to. One is the Aramaic version of the Lords Prayer and one is a prayer I wrote at the end of my Marian Retreat.

I have a more detailed way to meditate in this chapter.

Perhaps my favorite part of the 33 Day Marian Retreat was the part where one writes their own consecration to Mary and reads it every day. I began with the first paragraph given from the prayers to Mary and then wrote the following words to align with her Spirit.

"Mary, my Mother, I give myself totally to you as your possession and property.
Please make of me, of all that I am and have, whatever most pleases you.
Let me be a fit instrument in your immaculate and merciful hands for bringing
The greatest possible glory to God"

Beloved Mary, Queen of Angels
You who hold open heavens space.
Help me to have compassion
And forgiveness to heal the past
And bring me to your holy Grace.

Mary Holy Mother, I call upon your energy,
I ask you bring the Holy Spirit
To be alive inside of me.

Let me share the breath of your being
To live within the heart of God's great love,
I dedicate my path to the purpose
That you have shown for me to know.

With your tender understanding
You open up the door,
To the chosen one
And deliver me to the Lord.

Let me be anointed
By the holy waters from the source,
Let it quench my thirst for the beloved One
So I may serve as you would on Earth.

Be my guide and teacher
Let me honor the Light of your Golden Orb,
For the world's in needs of your mercy

Let my love help to bring it forth.

Bring the crown of stars you wear
Down to circle me,
Let me wear you're holy robe
So I can be surrounded with protection
To fulfill my destiny.

Let me breathe that holy spirit
Of the living light,
So I may be with God in the service
As a disciple in my life.

Allow the grace of your being
To transform my old mistaken ways,
Let your inspiration guide me to you
When I'm lost and know not what to do.

Holy mother full of Grace
Remove the binds of egos ties,
Unchain the limitations
And Free me from the lies.

Embrace me with your love
May I see your face in others I pray,
Let your life be an example
That inspires me ever day.

Speak with whispers to my soul
Let your precious words be shown,
To place upon life's altar
So I can offer them for others to know.

Thank you Holy Mother
For your patience and your grace,
Thank you Holy Spirit
For your presence that leads the way,
And guides me with patience and understanding every day.

Here is a translated form of the Lords Prayer, the Aramaic version by Jon Marc Hammer.)

Father–Mother of the cosmos, shimmering light of All,

Focus your light within us as we breathe your holy breath.
Enter the sanctuary of our hearts,
Uniting within us the sacred rays of your power and beauty.
Let your heart's desire unite Heaven and Earth through our sacred union.
Help us fulfill what lies within the circle of our lives today.
Forgive our secret fears, as we freely choose to forgive the secret fears of others.
Let us not enter into forgetfulness, tempted by false appearances.
For from your astonishing fire comes the eternal song
Which sanctifies all, renewed eternally in our lives and throughout creation.
We seal these words in our hearts, committed in trust and faith.

Prayers Sent by Heaven

There are these Prayers sent by Heaven
And the angels who watch over you,
With light that will heal
And give you the strength you need to renew.

The Prayers sent by Heaven
Are there to receive,
With Blessings so true
If you can just be open and believe.

So be still beloved
And take a few deep breaths,
And let the blessings of Heaven be
So you can share them with those in need.

These messages that come
On the wings of a dove,
Are there to inspire you
With the Mothers great love.

Let that love light guide you
And all that you do,
And bring you comfort
That will always get you through.

For Spirit speaks in so many ways
And you know this is true,
That is why we connect everyday.

There are lessons and guidance
There waiting for you,
So don't hold back or stop what you do
Have faith and allow the energy to continue.

There are prayers sent by heaven
So open up to your soul and receive,
The blessings that are waiting there
And Spirit will talk in so many ways to you.

Holy Mother

Holy Mother,
Divine Guardians of the Feminine
Principles of Love
Who have dedicated themselves to service,

I ask for the Gift of Healing
The Mind, Body and Heart.

May we truly forgive
The elements of abuse,
And restore the Power of Love;
May all of the pain and hurt suffered be released.

May we be baptized
By the pure understanding of the Feminine Spirit,
So that we may love ourselves
So we may love others.

May we accept this Love and Light
And truly feel the Amazing Grace
Of the Holy Spirit,
And the Radiant Light
From the Creator.

May the world be grateful for all the Women
Of Devotion who give so much on all levels of existence.
To our Mothers, and Mother Earth
And say, "Thank you for the gift of life",
And the many gifts of Love that bless us always.

Lord, teach me to be a better servant
So that I find a way to trust in you
And do all that you would need me to do,
And share these gifts you've given me to use.

May I Learn to be Humble

May I learn to be humble
For I have so much to learn,
And there are many things I thought I knew
That I might need to relearn.

There are so many here who can teach me
If I am open to hear and then,
Be aware of your presence
And have a beginners mind again.

And may I be reminded
That with your peace of mind,
What I need will come to me
And if I trust you will help me how to find.

That in this life there are so many ways
Your miracles are at work in life here,
I know that through your blessings
What I need will always appear.

And though I might not always see
What is waiting up the road,
I can have faith and trust
That with your help I will be shown.

How to be a humble servant
And be grateful for your great love,
And all the gift you've given me
To be open to the spirit of the Holy dove.

And my I find the truth the Mother brings
To fulfill my purpose in this life,
For I am but an instrument

To be play your song and share your light.

Meditation

After reading prayers that resonate with you go into meditation.
Meditation is one of the greatest gifts you can give yourself to transform your state of mind. People have been meditating since ancient times, and with a few basic techniques, you'll find that you, too, can come to a place of peace and relaxation.

Breath is the underlying principle of life. It carries your life force and is a very important aspect of meditation. Our thoughts often direct our breathing patterns, so use your breath to clear your mind before you meditate so you have a clean base from which to receive energy.

Breathe in light, and let it flow from the base of your spine up to your crown chakra at the top of your head. Breathe into the light and let it align your spine so that you are sitting comfortably with your back erect. Place your hands on your knees or cup them just below your navel.

This is a good point to recite an inspirational prayer to attune you to positive energies. Use powerful written words that lift your consciousness to a high vibration. I have included a selection of inspiring prayers for you to read at the end of the book. Choose any that work for you. Make sure you are receiving energy into your being without distraction.

Call upon Mother Mary to come to you. If you have any idea or question to share you send it out with love. Be aware that Mother Mary knows your concerns, she knows what is on your mind and in your heart. You are very visible to her as her beloved child. So be clear and open.

Be open to receive any messages that come from her. It might be as simple as a word or two. It might be a feeling.

Whatever it might be have a pen and paper handy to write down what comes in a Journal.

For me the messages come as poems. It may be a love letter of sorts or just a feeling of a lifting of energy. Whatever it might be, I honor it and am grateful for it. It is a gift and a blessing.

I have a deck of Doreen Virtue's Queen of Angels Cards, and I find it helpful to pull one if I want a message clarified.

The more you do this the more you feel comfortable with the process. It is a way to connect with Spirit and your soul. It a way you can use to listen and hear the calling.

Here are some messages that you can use as seed meditations.

Speak With Spirit

If you could speak with the breath of spirit
And let your soul be heard,
Would it be a true resonance of the light
The essence of the Divine Presence here in life?

The word of God is sacred
And we share it in this energy where we live,
It is alive the song the birds design
It is in the heart of the cry of Love Divine.

It is in the chorus of the music
The hallelujah sung at the break of Easter morn,
It is in the ringing of the bells you hear
That summon you to prayer.

Yes you can hear the word of God
In the scriptures verse you read,
The word of God is a frequency
That carries a Divine Energy.

And what is the word of God?
And how do you capture it and define
The power of creation
That holds such secrets for us to find?

Right in this very moment you can hear
If you listen in silence with care,
You might just find
The word of God is Love Divine.

May Mary's Messages of Love Speak to You

May Mary's messages of love guide you
And open your heart to be
In service to the Mother,
A channel for her pure energy.

We are given the gifts of heaven
They are there if we believe,
There is such abundant blessings
Alive in the bliss she brings.

The world is now awakening
To the power of the Divine Mother's Light
That is alive within each soul,
Grace can provide a way for us to know.

If we are receptive
We each can find,
The gift of this loving energy
With compassion and peace for all humankind.

So open your heart
And go deep within,
Allow the presence to be with you
And let the blessings begin.

The Mother Speaks

The Mother speaks
If we can listen, just listen, we can hear,
The messages from the Mother
Speak to us so loud and clear.

In ways that we sometimes can't even see
With protection and her Divine Mercy,
The Mother speaks and guides us to what is right
And those we pray for who need help
In their lives.

The Mother speaks, the Mother speaks
Listen,
And you can hear
The power of the Mother's Love,
At work every moment of your life my dear.

Give great thanks be grateful for
The blessing she brings,
That help us to restore
By faith and ways we might not even see.
Believe the Mother speaks
For the Mother speaks to me.

She brings Her Faith,
She brings Her Grace,
She brings us everything we need
To make our lives more loving.

So we can share messages of the Mother
That deliver Her Blessings,
So listen close so loud and clear
For in you heart if love so deep,
You can hear the Mother speak.

Many times messages and Divine Communication will happen when we are asleep.
Dreams are often a way our masters and teachers try to reach out to us.
You might want to keep a journal handy by your bedside and write down what comes to you.

The Awakened Dream

And while the world was sleeping
The Angels were preparing the way,
The masters knew the time had come
For the world to evolve to the next stage.

The heavenly choirs were singing
Many prayers where being prayed,
And the Queen of Angels had taken her throne

To send forth love from her Holy place.

The Lord on high had spoken
And the time was finally at hand,
For the world to finally awaken
And evolve to the next level for man.

And there was a great sense of change
As the grand architect held the plans,
The blueprint was already done
To reflect heavens holy space.

And the dreamers dream was being fulfilled
And many on earth could see,
A change in the grand vision
A graduation to a higher reality.

And there was a grand celebration
And there was a joy of such grace,
And heaven was finally merged with earth
And the dreamer's dream was embraced.

And a great light shone forth from heaven
Upon the planet Earth,
And from the Highest mountain tops
The Holy call went forth.

Great beams of radiance touched all hearts
And love smiled forth blessings upon all mankind,
The sound of the sacred word was heard
For creation was now awakening to a new world.

And we all felt the power of God
And understood the higher plan,
And we found that heaven
Could be brought to the world.
And we could now graduate
With the help of enlightened men,

The awakened world is not just a dream my friend
It has become a reality,
Believe in the power of love and light
And see that this is our destiny.

You can embody the dreamers dream
The one who awakens the world.
And we can all work together
To bring this vision heaven on earth,
With Light Love and peace
To become our new reality.

The Heartbeat of Love

Listen, listen to the symphony of life,
For if you listen you can hear
The heartbeat alive in each blessed breath of light,
And the love that feeds its presence here.

You can tune in to the pulse of humanity
As it vibrates with each frequency so clear,
The Earth is speaking to us in each moment,
Through the water in the oceans, through the air,
And all the creatures who abide here.

If you listen you can hear
The music of the universe,
Alive in the energy,
Alive throughout the spheres.

You can hear the heartbeat of the cosmos
As it dances with dark and light,
Each star's song is alive
With its own destiny in life.

The Master answers our prayers,
Although sometimes it's hard to tell,
But if we rest our head upon his chest,
We may hear the heartbeat of love.

Brilliant symphonies of life sounds,
Sweet callings of each and every breath,
Merge us with the harmony of the universe,
As the song of life infinitely plays.

Listen, listen for God's energy,
As it speaks freely in blessings that abound,
In the heartbeat of the symphony of sounds,
Alive in us as the music of love.

The Calling

Radiant Blissful Light of the Presence
I breathe with the One breath of life,
I redeem my heritage and destiny
I allow every atom of the
Pure Love that you are,
To fill my Body, Mind and Soul.

For you are my purpose
You are my very being,
And I accept this Love
That holds the core of my soul,
To open and receive
And forgive all the barriers of fear.

So I may be a Pure Vessel and Channel of the Source
For you are the Gift of Who I am,
And You hold the Perfect Peace
That is the resolution of misunderstanding.

With you I may see myself anew
And rededicate my purpose to serve.

Bless this dream and the Awakening
As I in turn bless the journey of the One Source with all life,
The foundation and creation that is a living reality
Alive with this breath,
In this perfect moment of now.

Journal Writing

Writing a journal of your spiritual journey with Mary is a very good practice. When you meditate you are mentally and spiritually traveling to inner realms and many experiences will occur in that sacred time. By writing down any reflections or messages that come from inner states of awareness you can strengthen the conscious awareness of any subtle experiences that occur.

It is handy to have a pen and journal, that has been blessed in the light available so that you can record any experiences that occur.

By writing down your impressions from your soul you also develop the inner thread of awareness that exists from the inner consciousness to the outer.

After having established a pattern of writing down these recollections it becomes easier and easier to do. There still can exist times when you wonder and doubt if the messages will come and that is when faith and belief in your self can come into play. The mind becomes more sensitive and trained to be able to receive inner impressions to relate to outer consciousness the more you practice doing it.

You will also get inspired by what you get as messages and this will encourage you to continue the practice. Here are some steps you can follow to get into a meditative sate for Journal writing

1. Follow these steps.
2. Do deep clearing breaths
3. Go to the inner place of the Soul consciousness
4. Dwell in the center of the Soul's Light
5. Make an inner connection with your higher self or guide
6. Ask if there are any messages or ask your question
7. Wait in a receptive silence for impressions or messages
8. While in the Light of the Soul, write down messages in your journal
9. Read back what you have written
10. Sound an inner "ohm" and return to meditation
11. Say "Thank you God"

Sometimes you will actually hear an inner voice relay messages to you and sometimes you will not feel as if anything has come, or maybe just one word will come. When this happens have faith and still pick the pen and begin writing anyway. Sometimes the process of writing triggers the messages. The inner impressions will vary with your ability to receive clear connection with your guide or higher self. At certain times, like the full moon you may find it easier to make that connection and to be inspired.

By writing in your Journal you will develop an inner form of communication with your inner guide and higher self. Sometimes answers will come right away and other times you might get an answer later. It is a true resource for your teaching and guidance from Mother Mary.

Journal writing is a wonderful tool for inner development and it acts as a way of record keeping of your spiritual journey and it reflects your time spent with your Higher self and guides. It can be a great gift from the Mother and a true blessing from God.

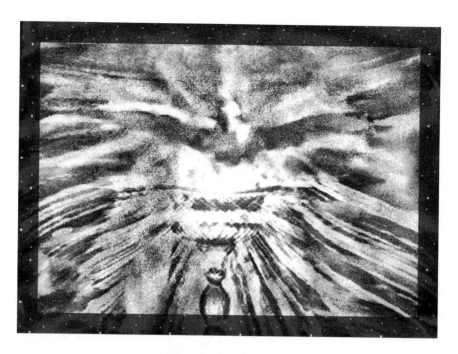

. Here in the Magnificence
Where dark meets Light,
We exist as the key to a universe
A feather on the breath in flight.

There is a wonder of the All in All
That is the gateless gate,
That leads to the realms that hold the very moment
Of conception with an enlightenment of our soul

Chapter 6
Giving and Receiving

Every man shall give as he is able, according to the blessing of the LORD
your God which He has given you.- Deuteronomy 16:17

The Divine Mother is the giver of Life. She gave life to Jesus Christ, She
gives her love and miracles to the world. It is no mistake we call this planet
Mother Earth, for she is a receiver of all of our energies, and a giver of life
to us all. She feeds us, from Her we are clothed, and we breathe Her air,
drink form Her water. She blesses with Her endless gifts here.

Are we open to receive the gifts She gives?

What vibration or energy are you giving people? What are you putting
out to the World? Is it positive? Does it carry light and love? If it is, it acts
like a magnet that attract the light and love back.

What energy are you receiving? And if it's negative, how do you react or
not react to it? Can you just observe? Can you transform that energy into a
higher perspective and understand what's really going on?

If the angels in heaven were to tune into your frequency what would
they be hearing? What are you broadcasting out to the world? For what you
send out is what you're get back. Giving and receiving and what you choose
to be is your choice. It is so helpful to think of what the Mother is giving
and try for a moment to serve that unconditional love.

We are like radio stations tuned into certain channels of energy. We can
tune into the Love channel, and pick up the positive energy and beauty of

the world, or we can be broadcasting the channel of bad news and negativity. We can choose to be victims of life or see all the blessing we have.

It really is similar to just breathing. It's similar to breathing in, which is you receiving your breath of life, and breathing out, and releasing that breath. When you breathe in, hold it for a second, and let that energy, that moment, that pause at the top of your breath, fill you with that beautiful energy, the Ha the breath of life. And when you breathe out, you release it all the way out, and you let that energy be released out into the universe.

It is important to think and meditate about what we are giving and what we are receiving in life. Are we serving the Lord, are we serving love. Bob Dylan wrote a great song called, "You've Gotta Serve Somebody." We all do even if we are not aware of it. Are we serving our Ego or our we serving our Higher Presence?

I find that I need to take time every morning to recommit myself to Mother Mary's path. And then to do inner check-ins during the day. I find it helpful to reflect at night what was the day's energy like. Was it loving and kind, or full of stress and strife?

Also it's important to know if you are in balance with what you give and what you receive.

Questions For Reflection

Go to a quiet place or your alter. Sit and light a candle. Have a journal and pen handy.

Ask yourself some of these questions and then after meditating on them write down what you find.

Are you someone who is giving all the time or are you someone who takes?

What do you give and why do you give?

Do you like to give or receive?

Do you feel worthy to receive?

What are you receiving?

What would you like to receive more of?

One of God's great gifts is the beauty this world displays. Do you see the beauty in life?

How could you take time to see more beauty?
What are you blessed by in your life?

How are you a blessing to others?
Write down some of your blessings.
Do you feel like a Victim?

Are you grateful for your life and the gifts life gives you?

Light Exercise

Create a space where you can be in communion with God.
Direct your consciousness to the higher realms of Heaven.
In an infinite flow of light visualize two living stream of energy coming down in a giant V.
See one stream of energy from Father God and One from Mother God.
See the V of light coming down to your heart. There is activates the energy with your heart to bring the love in your heart center to a revitalized power.
Now see a flow of circular energy flow on down the rest of your body in pillars of gold.
Do this three times.

Here are some messages about giving, receiving and the beauty.

What Are You Giving and Receiving?

In life what is given can be taken
With every breath there's a blessing given,
The receiving and releasing
All particles of creation making
Beings of illusion of our own creation
Just a dream in the awakening.

And Jesus gave his life,
The lamb of God's sacrifice was taken
To show us that in life we find,
We are just a temporary form in time.

But we can live forever and be reborn,
Spirit released to eternity to be delivered to a new form;
This earthly gift we can receive
'Til we live and learn and then are released.

And at this time of year we see
The cycles of the seasons so clear;
Spring comes with the flowers so dear
Sunrise on Easter to reflect resurrection here.

And we can learn to forgive
Ourselves and those lost as Jesus did;
And we can behold the light and awake
To the love all that life gives and takes.

Giving and Receiving

Oh, we give and give and give
To try to share our hearts and souls;
Always reaching higher and higher
To reach that ultimate goal.

And sometimes we steal from heaven
To try to capture a little of the beauty there;
To bring it back to the place we live,
Trying to hold a piece of the glory
While we are living here.

And there is such good we've experienced
Behind heavens doors,
We search to find it in our life
But feel an emptiness inside.

There is that place in our hearts
That was once torn apart
And needs to be restored;
And we try to always hide
How that heart needs so much love to survive.

And yet we can't believe
That we are good enough to receive
The love we really need,

That will bring us to be healed.

All this giving
Is just a part of the process
Of the love that it seems we can't receive.

If we go running after the promise
We gave to God so long ago,
Can we get back to that place
We started from
And once again be made whole?

It's so hard to manage it gets to the point one day
'Til you just stop and have to decide
To be present with yourself,
And what's there inside your heart and mind.

It all comes down to acceptance
Of yourself and others you find,
It's just a point to get to
With true honesty inside;
Something that is there and you know it
And yet it's so hard to define.

The greatest gift you can get
Is just being able to be yourself you see,
For who is it that is giving
In what is it that you need to be.

Accept God's unconditional love inside you,
That is the greatest gift you can receive.

Are You Open to Receive?

Are you open to receive God's blessings?
Can you find it in yourself, find the power
To reach up and touch the face of God
And see Creation in the soul you are?

And what is gained and what is lost
In accepting the truth that you find,
Are you able to believe and discover

What the Teacher of Life does hold?
Are you open to be the blessings you're given?
Do you find yourself worthy to see?
That the heart that is open to love is fed
From the energy from the source and will set you free.

Receive the Presence of this Precious Light
Be the Presence of this gift of Love,
Become the living blessing
Of God's greatest gift alive in your soul.

For the gifts of the Universe are given for free
If you own the power to receive them,
In the realms of your very being
You can give and so receive.

Such a Wonder

Such a wonder this life brings,
Such a sacred song to sing;
Fallen feathers drop here
A way Angels let us know they are there.

Beyond the sky where Spirit lies
This mystery is redeemed;
For some understanding of how to be
Present here across the shore.

Such a wonder this life brings,
Such a sacred song to sing;
A butterfly dances in the morning light
Circling round to gently remind.

We are dwelling here in time and space,
In this splendid dream that we have made;
Until we find we need more
Then we knock on our souls door.

And who is there to greet our gaze
When we finally see God face-to-face?
That mask that we create falls away
'Til naked we embrace Infinite Love's embrace.

With such a wonder this life brings,
Such a sacred song to sing;
So many gift's of God's great blessing
To prove Spirit lives in everything.

A Reflection of God's Beauty

I am a beam of the Light of God's Creation
That flows from the Source to the soul,
Here for a while on this planet
As the very breath of living love.

I am a servant of God's energy
Living, breathing, working to prepare,
This blessed Holy Spirit here in form
That learns as it seeks to share.

The reflection of this beauty
The sounds of Spirit in the Holy Word,
All part of the living river of life
Blessed by of God's unconditional love.

It pours from the source
As the perfect imperfection
That listens sometimes and hears,
The sound of the cosmic vibrations
That reverberates within the body here.

We dream of love,
We hunger for light
In the vision that redeems,
For a part of our spirit that lives forever
Is granted by eternity.

We work with their fellow humans
To lift our hearts together as one,
And with compassion as our guide
We understand our purpose to become.

The reason why we are here
To serve God with our love,

Which we must find in others
And is also inside the heart of us.

Listen

Listen and hear the calling
That comes at the break of dawn,
It whispers to my soul
And brings me to that power
To believe that we can always grow.

I am the living Light of Love,
I am that I am
Alive here in this body mind and soul,
The breadcrumbs of the holy communion.

I am the one who thirsts
To merge with the lord,
A watercolor daydream that fades
With lightning bolts that flash with possibilities
As the breath of the wind
Asks me to worship you with praise.

I am the breath of wind
That blows forth from the ocean,
To reach the stormy skies,
To feed my hungry soul
With the gifts it can't define.

I am the budding flower
That shimmers with beauty so divine,
And opens up to the sun
To blossoms when love comes by.

I am touched with the smile of masters love
With a promise yet to find.

So I eat the message
That the fortune cookie holds
And it says:
"You are you, And I am I,
We all will awaken in Gods good time".

Beyond the limitations of this life
I see the merging of the one,
Creation's manifestation awakening
To the "I Am" that causes us to become.

That living Light of Love
Alive in our body mind and soul,
The awakening that comes to us
From the holy ones above.

Can You See the Beauty?

Can you see the Beauty
Of the grace that Blesses you when you pray?
Can you embody the Holy Spirit
That brings this gift your way?

Can you really feel
The good that God does bring?
With the presence of the Holy Mother
And her compassion that holds us in Presence of her being.

You are part of this one Light,
You are part of the Holy Heart
That holds us all in such a loving space;
As you find our way through the illusion of this earthly place.

Can you see the Beauty
Of the Light surrounding you?
And the grace that comes and blesses you
That is forever there to help and to renew.

Can you really see the way
That she does see into the depths of your hidden heart?
To help you when we are in need
And save you with the smile she brings.

For there is such a purity
And there is this heavenly glow,
That she extends out to you
As she blesses you to know.

If you can just love yourself enough
To forgive the mistakes you've made,
And then really feel the depths of compassion
And the power to live with the love it takes.

So ask for the amazing grace to come and hold you tight
And bring the blessings of Divine Love,
So that you can be healed and make things right.

Find a way to believe
That you can make a brand new start,
You can be living with the blessings
Of the love that she brings into your heart.

Magnificence

Here in the Magnificence
Where dark meets Light,
We exist as the key to a universe
A feather on the breath of flight.

There is a wonder of the All in All
That is the gateless gate,
That leads to the realms that hold our very moment
Of conception and comprehension an enlightenment of our sight.

And we hold the key to reach the All within us
If we can just encompass
The Soul's Eternal existence as it exists touching heaven and earth
With each rebirth is really a Magnificent thing.

For beyond the beyond
Is within the within,
And the space where they meet
Is this power of pure energy alive in everything.

We are given reasons that we understand
The Love that brought us here.

And this Pure Energy is the springboard

For us to find the key for our enlightenment,
Just out of reach and yet always right here.

Be in this divine moment
And allow your soul to experience the kiss of bliss
In all of the depths and heights of your being.
Alive and present as a key to the Magnificence
Here in the eternal now present where you are.

To receive energy you must be able to be still and receptive. All of the sensory receptors should be open and attuned to the Light. Any issues of unworthiness that arise should be released so that you can be open to God's Light and Love. This is a time to recharge those batteries and be renewed.

You are a child of God born of Light and Love. You are one with that energy so receive that energy and be made whole and new by it. Be open and allow the pure energy to come to you. Accept that energy and let it be at home in your being. The more you feel open to receive the more you allow others to give. Also, the more you can give from your true self.

Give with the worthiness of your heart and Soul, not as a deflection of energy away from you. For sometimes givers do deflect energy by being the initiator and using their own power to control and give. As you receive more, the more you can be grateful for what you get. And you will begin to understand that.

Giving and receiving are of the same energy flow. You will find you can truly give from your soul with Unconditional Love and Light when you receive from "who you are".

Your life becomes a "Yes, Yes, Yes, Yes" to God's Light, "Yes" to God's Love, "Yes" to life and living, "Yes" to the process of sending and receiving pure energy; "Yes" to the whole of it all. "Yes" to what you ask for and "Yes" to giving forth the blessing of positive energy flowing through you to yourself and to others. "Yes" to the entire creative process of the Universe.

And when you say "Yes" to God, God says "Yes" to you. Thank-you God for it all.

The soul knows this love that has a home
In the energy with which Mother brings forth life,
And it can work and grow and blossom
In seeds planted that reflect pure light.

Each breath of love blossoms with the smile of beauty,
And each smile of love helps heal the broken heart,
And each heart that is open can understand
That love is the greatest gift God gives.

Chapter 7
Love

Love is patient, love is kind. It does not envy, it does not boast, it is not proud. It does not dishonour others, it is not self-seeking, it is not easily angered, it keeps no record of wrongs. Love does not delight in evil but rejoices with the truth. It always protects, always trusts, always hopes, always perseveres.
(Corinthians 13:4-8)

I experienced a union with God when I was 15 years old.
It was an experience that changed my life forever. I actually left my body and went to the higher realms of light until I made contact with God and felt the most powerful unconditional love that I had ever known then or since then.
This love is not the kind of love that can truly be expressed in words. How do words capture the light of love? How can we understand the power of love? God's Love was experienced when Mother Mary united with him and merged with his spirit.

It is through our personal experience that we see love, know love, fall in love and learn from love.
Love is the underlying principle of all life. It is unconditional love that God expressed through Christ. Mother Mary's love shows us that we can embody love. Love can redeem our lives. It is our divine inheritance, our salvation and gift.

As we embrace love in its many disguises, we feel the living energy of God's love, which is eternal. God is the Source of all life and God's love is alive in all life.

When we love God we can learn to love ourselves, and when we love ourselves, we can receive love from others. In this now moment, say yes to love and be grateful for the power of love in your life.

Love is so gentle and kind. Many of us have grown up in a world where it takes a lot of energy, and sometimes even a lot of willpower, to get things done. It's just like you almost have to sometimes try to meet this pretty, pretty strong energy, to meet it, to not be overwhelmed by it. But the answer is not to try to use your own willpower, but to turn it all over to God's will. And I have recently just come back to that again, and again, and again, every morning now in meditation, asking for God's will to be done. And when you let God's will and the Mother's will work through you, there's this balance of love and will that will get done without you having to be stressed, without having to be aggressive, without having to fight for yourself as you do sometimes in life, these days especially; you give it over. And I do this prayer where I let myself be a servant to Mary every morning

If anytime anything comes up, just always take a breath and just say, "Love, love, love,"

The Mother keeps reminding us there is no other than love. We're all her children and there's no evidence she has favorites. Jesus said, "All those who love and do the will of my Father, all those who love and do the will of the infinite, this is my family, these are my brothers and sisters," and that's what we would say to everyone. We're all a part of the great humanity, and everyone who wakes up... the Mother has a very gentle sweet call. It's so good to know that all your sins, or mistakes are forgiven and released. It is an ongoing process, so you may have to repeatedly remember to forgive and release, for you are overcoming habits and attitudes of a lifetime.

We are able through love to reach all the keys to the kingdom of heaven within.

It may take daily vigilance and maintenance to remember to use these tools we are given. The time given to returning to love is well worth it. Love is the answer to every problem. Choosing love has rewards in more ways then you might know, not just in this life but after you leave this body and return home.

Love Exercise and Visualization

Visualize yourself sitting in a beautiful garden in Heaven. There is a lovely fragrance of flowers, the sound of water running in the streams, and birds singing and flying overhead.

You are surrounded in a field of light with pillars of light surrounding you. Be at one with the light around you. Feel the peace that passeth understanding. Know that all is well.

You are able to sense the fragrance of roses.

Hundreds of petals fall through the air in shades of pink. Your heart smiles and you feel unconditional love.

She comes before you and stands in front of you in the Garden. She sends you pure unconditional love spiraling into your heart of hearts. There deep in the heart of Heaven's Garden, a Golden Rose is planted and grows. She picks the Rose and hands it to you. You now send your love back out to her with a spiraling energy of the pure love she gave back, to her. This continues until the entire garden is lit with divine love. You are now the light of Mary's love. As you come out of the time in the Garden know that you can always return to this, your place in Mary's Garden of Love.

Love, Love and Love

Again and again return to love, my friend,
For as you bring your life to love solutions
You have a fertile field with which you can
Live and grow your soul's life purpose.

For the soul knows this love that has a home
In the energy with which Mother brings forth life,
And it can work and grow and blossom
In seeds planted that reflect pure light.

Each breath of love blossoms with the smile of beauty,
And each smile of love helps heal the broken heart,
And each heart that is open can understand
That love is the greatest gift God gives.

For spirit dwells in the heart of living love,
And the light of this spirit holds the pure reflection
Of God-spirit merging in man.
As Earth and humanity bring this love to life,
We become the consciousness of the living love of God,
We become co-creators who live in the light of God's love

We can feed the fire of the Holy Spirit
With the fuel of our lives,
For every time we choose love,
We choose the resource God gave us for life.
We can find passion for our life's purpose,
And compassion for those who suffer in the process
Of learning how to forgive and live with love.

So breathe the light of love into your heart,
For it holds your true purpose here in life.
The Mother delivers you to accept
We are the perfect imperfection the reason for being alive.

Golden Flower of Love

Let the divine rays of God's Golden Light
Open the flower
Within the temple of the heart.

The heart's pure attunement to the Light
Calls forth energy it needs to blossom,
At the dawn's calling,
To the golden Flower of Love.

Feel the heart come alive
In the radiance of being,
And let the joy of this glorious gift
Fill you with the perfect light of love.

Precious Flower of Love,
The sacred rose of the Mother Divine
You have your roots in the Source of all life,
And you are joined to all hearts in love.

You are the soul's gift alive in Spirit,
Opening the heart,
The temple of Living Love.

You are from seeds in heaven's garden,
Rooted in the healing love
That awakens the beauty
That lives within us, here on earth.

We bow before you in all your beauty,
And offer you in love,
For others to see the perfection living within us,
As the golden Flower of Love

The Holy Light of the Madonna's Love

In the Holy Light of the Madonna's Love
A radiance shines forth to you,
And softly she reaches out and speaks
These words ring out so true.

Come all ye who are pure of heart
And let your soul be seen,
Come all who seek my refuge here
And I'll provide you sweet sanctuary.

Come all who are broken-hearted,
Come all who have suffered with fear.
Come all who are so weary,
I'll provide you peace in a safe space here.

Cleanse away the past mistakes
With the holy waters from the Source,
Purify your past mistakes and ask to start anew.
Let all of the old ways go,
And allow your self to be renewed.

In the holy light of the Mothers gaze
There is the power for you to see,
What is in the depths of your soul
With a promise of a better life to be.

There is a saving grace here
And she provides you with her protection,
With a sacred space to pray
To find a Higher Way and she does say.

Come all ye who in need of comfort,
Come to this holy place.

Where the lord dwells in his kingdom
And dwells throughout all time and space.

I will provide you comfort,
You will find such great peace.
You will find the love here waiting
And forgiveness will set you free.

The Path of Love

The path of Love is not always easy
But have hope and do not despair.
For with love your heart may be torn open
But when you heart is open there is room
For the true love of God to be there.

Thus love will lift up when you are broken
And when you are down on your knees,
You might just ask for help and find
That gift of the power of love inside.

And you can forgive the hurt that has come to you,
You can forgive the mistakes you made.
And forgive all the things you had to do,
And you can put aside your pride.

For you are never forsaken
And if you are open and ask for help,
You will not be denied.

For there is a greater love that can teach you
To believe in the love inside that is true,
And if you ask you can be healed,
And it is this love that can overcome the fear you knew.

For the greatest power is in the love inside you
And it is a blessing that we all should receive,
For you are the living love of God
And that love can set you free.

So celebrate this day of Love

By forgiving any hurt in your heart.
And believe once again that love is worthwhile
So you can dedicate this day to make a new start.

And maybe get your self a special gift or a card
To recognize the love that you are,
There in your heart of hearts.

And make it a point to share your love
With the ones who are sad and have been torn apart,
For there is a flame that burns in your soul
That is lit when you let love be in control.

And take a moment to thank those you loved
And realize that love can overcome fear,
And you are able to love yourself
For love is the reason that you are here.

Love Yourself

Love yourself for who you are,
Love your mind, body and your soul.
Love yourself as God loves you,
Any blocks placed there by you can always be removed
So that you can fulfill your life true goals.

You have the power of unlimited love in you
And it will give you the strength if you believe,
You can accomplish what ever you choose
You can be whatever you want to be.

If you just love yourself beloved one
And serve that love to see,
You can change your life with this love
To bring joy to your life and fulfill your destiny.

Love yourself beloved one,
Love yourself and you'll see how
This love will change your life,
This love will heal your mind.

This love is here right now,
Receive the blessings that are waiting,
That are there in this very moment right now.

Breathe it into your heart to find,
Absorb it into each and every cell,
Let all the love that you need
Come to you so you can find out how.

You are perfect in your imperfections,
You are the best that you can be,
You are unique and one of a kind,
Release all limitations believe and you will see
You can love yourself enough to know.
This Unconditional love will set you free.

The Power of the One Light

You can be in tune with the Universe
And the power of the one Light,
The very source of all creation
Is alive and there to experience inside.

And what you do with this gift
And what you choose to perceive,
Is up to you to decide
And is based in how much you believe.

So open up your heart
And let the love light in,
And let the soul connect you
To power of God within.

Be in tune with the universe
And the magic that is alive,
And find that perfect energy
That aligns you with the One Universal Mind.

Life does not have to be a struggle
When you connect with the energy of the Source,
And when you are in tune with the Universe

You can be able to comprehend what you are here for.

So let the power of the Presence
Be alive in your soul,
And let the soul guide you
To discover the way to know.

How to let life be a blessing
So you can share the beauty you find,
And you can be in tune with the Source of all
And help to serve humankind.

Love As I Love

The Christ said, "Love as I love",
And believe enough in yourself
To let it connect you to God's love,
And let God's love live within you.

Love as I love,
And experience the radiant energy of
Unconditional love that heals as it reveals.
Allow that love to enter your heart,
And be alive within you,
As the spirit of God is present within me.
And see that same presence of love
Within the heart of others too.

Love as I love,
And allow it to be in you,
As an infinite flow of energy
From the Source of all that is true.

Love as I love,
And let that love teach you and lead you,
So you may see love and feel love,
And learn from the power of this love.

Love as I love,
And let it live through all time and space.
Call upon that love that God shares with all life.

Call upon the way of love,
And feel it at work in your heart, mind and body,
And let God's love shine through you as eternal light.

Love as I love,
And become the love of God,
And as I am that love of God,
So that you may be the love of God,
For it is your reason for being.

Love as I love,
For this is God's love,
And it is alive in you,
Now and always let it be your true resonance.

Sweet Love Of The Mother

Sweet love of the Mother
Let the spark of light within my soul,
Be ablaze with the eternal fire
That is of your spirit to know.

May Divine Love teach me to believe
In my heart of hearts,
That a sacred gift you have given me.

It feeds my faith,
And nourishes my life.
And this love is alive in me
In this very moment to receive.

When I try and try in my mind
To justify the how's and why's
And humbly accept that
You are the Way, the Truth and the Life.

May I drink from the sacred chalice of spirit's Source,
May I breathe in the life force of redemption,
May I offer what I have to serve
The great I AM that I AM

As I walk on the path,
And find the blessing here on earth,
I see your love and light,
I pray your true reflection is in my life.

Learning to Serve Love

It's important to remember,
Sometimes we can't make it on our own,
And if we ask for a little help,
We must welcome it when it comes.

And when we ask to be of service,
If we get a chance to serve,
We should learn to love that service,
For it's just what we have asked for.

And if we ask for help, we can't be surprised
When it comes knocking at our door,
So we just go and are happy,
And recognize what it came for.

For we are given a chance to choose
The way we wish to be.
We can be angry, freaked out, or loving,
But if we ask for help, we must be able receive.

To really make a difference
In the way we live our lives,
We must be willing to make some changes
That can lead us out of strife.

And if we wish to serve,
We must embrace what comes our way,
And let the One we wish to serve
Teach us how to do it better each day.

So when we ask for help,
Trust it's on the way,
Let the Queen Of Angels will come to guide us,
No matter what we do or say.

If we can find the strength to serve,
We'll find that many lessons come,
But we must first put aside our egos,
And let Father Mother God's love come and see us through.

How Do You Hold This Precious Jewel?

How do you hold this precious jewel
Diamond that your heart holds?
Do you feel the spirit of the soul
That burns away the fear we know?

How do you let your life truly shine,
And allow it to be
A true reflection of the cosmos
Spinning throughout infinity?

You are part of stars of such great light
A precious jewel that shines so bright,
You are a reflection of God's Love Divine
Breathing in tune to the secrets still undefined.

Release and forgive what cannot be told,
Let this healing come to show.
This precious diamond of the soul
Calls your heart to blossom and grow.

And sometimes life can reveal
If you can just try to believe,
There is an exquisite beauty to see
This priceless gift given for free.

Just this thing we call Love Divine
That we always seek for and try to define,
This jewel in our heart of God's Great Light
This diamond reflecting the Spirit of Christ.

If You Can Love Yourself

If you can love yourself,
You will find the key.
Love yourself as the Holy Mother would
Believe you are worthy to receive.

If you can just release
The past and all that happened long ago,
You can learn to love again
And let that love fill your body, mind, and soul.

Come into the Presence
Of the Divine Grace that she provides,
And let your Self be healed
And find that place where Joy resides.

Believe this in your heart of hearts
Allow yourself to feel this in your soul,
Miracles are possible
If you pray for help you will know.

If you have faith you will be blessed
And be touched by the Grace,
As you look into the Holy Mother's face behold
The Love of God there shows.

So listen in the silence
And pray for the power to hear,
The guidance that you need
Will always then appear.

Offer her your love
And forgive yourself so you may truly love too.
Believe that you are worthy
And give thanks for the blessings,
She shows to me and you

You Are Loved

When the world brings no solutions
All through the darkest night,
When the soul has lost connection
To what was once so right.

Call upon the angels
Who listen deep inside,
Call upon the Guiding Light
It's there that you will find.

You can find the Answers
To what you need to know,
To take you through the doorway
And find the Peace within your soul.

You are a child of the Universe
Your destiny is clear,
You are blessed more than you may know
True joy is oh so near.

Call upon the Spirit
Of the Holy ones,
If you fall they're waiting
To lead you on the journey that you're on.

So stop and open up your heart
And they will speak to you,
Listen for the words of Truth
And they will see you through.

You are not alone out there
You are loved, so find
A way to believe again
A way to heal the mind.

You are loved by God,
You are Light Divine.
You are a Child of the Universe,
Claim this truth and you will find,

You are Loved by God,

Feel this love and be redeemed,
Forgive those who hurt you,
Forgive yourself and all your mistaken deeds.

Precious Flower of Love

You are a Precious Flower of Love,
A Blessed Blossom of Light above.
Born from a seed of Heaven's Garden and
Given unto Heavens Gate by the Creator's Son.

We can plant the seed of a flower or tree
So in our heart this love will grow,
Bring this gift of beauty to those
Who would care for it and know.

You are now a precious Flower of Heaven
With all of the elements you have given as gifts.
Still here with roots in the earth, kissed by breath of the air,
Blessed rain from skies and the fire whose brilliance is light's rebirth.

Bring the perfect reflection of Spirit
In the beauty that we all now know.
For all the earth is single flower,
And we all hold this magic in our soul.

So if God were to offer you this Perfect Gift
Of a seed of a Flower from Heaven's Garden to grow,
Could you open your heart and accept it
And care for the perfection that unfolds?

For we all are Precious Flowers of Love,
When in Heaven and when we find rebirth.
You were brought here to care for the Garden
So Paradise can be remembered by your time on earth.

Care for the Love inside you,
Care for the seeds you plant,
Share the Gift of the Garden of Heaven
And bring that love right back here to Earth.

A Rose of the Heart

A rose of the heart
Blossoms with Love,
A thing of Pure Beauty
Blessed by Heaven above.

The thorns that you've placed
For your protection that are there,
You find now block the gift within
That you came here to share.

The flower of such Grace is pure
Beyond the mind's confines,
And a gift so beautiful that words fail to define
The blessings that inspire this our hearts lifeline.

The petals so fragile
Softly to earth do fall,
And we try to catch their beauty this moment
And the hope and innocence it recalls.

To remove the thorns takes such trust I know
So we call on the angels who always stand by
And they shower their spirit's intent
And bring us a vision of Paradise so radiantly sent.

A rose of the Heart
Lies there within you,
Remove the thorns
And let angels of Christ's see you through.

Let these petals of love fall as they may,
You cannot hold onto what is gone, try as you may.
Surround yourself with the One who Created this Dream
A Rose without Thorns is a Heavenly thing.

Receive the Beauty and the Love
That God has given so freely from above,
And enjoy the mystery of beauty of life you see,
And offer the Rose in Your Heart at the Alter of God
In thanks for your life and the love you received.

Let The Blessings Begin

Simply say "Yes" to the Infinite Love
That the Christ spirit radiates,
And let it unfold within your heart.
For in this perfect moment of allowance,
The love that is the spirit of God is waiting,
In an infinite field of perfect energy.

We can meet there and bring
The love that is within us
Into our hearts and souls, into our very being.
This love is my love, and God's gift to you.

This love is your teacher and your guide,
This love is a precious jewel,
And it causes the light that you are to shine,
With the brilliance of a thousand suns.

This love is the perfect flower that blossoms,
And intoxicates your senses so that you are lifted
To the garden of Heaven.
This love is the Truth of God, and it is my truth.

Would you behold the joy that this love brings?
Would you put a price on a love such as this?
And how would you celebrate this love
That is given to you unconditionally and freely?
Would you say Yes to this love?
Would you allow yourself to believe in this love?
Would you open up your heart and soul
To this love that God is and I am?

For you are this love,
And I am alive as the Christ in this love.
This love is waiting for you to open the door to your heart,
And say "Yes" to the love that is right there within you.

Embrace this love, breathe in this precious love,
And let its flame burn bright with the Eternal Light
That will guide you and lead you

To find the Way, the Truth and the joy,
In this perfect now moment, when you choose
The love that I am and you are.

Holy Mother of Love

Holy Mother, blessed one of God
And let us feel the power your love can bring,
And with love we praise you
With these words we sing.

Thank-you to the Highest,
We thank you and we pray
That we may with Grace be guided
To bring Heaven to earth someday.

Meditation On Love

This meditation not only brings you the delicious feeling of the Golden Light of Love, it can also affect the space you are in and people around you such as on an airplane, at home, at work, or any other place you might be.

Sit in a quiet place and go into a peaceful place of silence within.

Breathe slowly and deeply in and out. Let each breath relax you and bring you further into yourself.

Each breath brings you light from the Highest Light of God. See this light come down through your head. Let it bring you a smile of joy.

Bathe in the joy and love.

Breathe in again and feel any tension in your shoulders dissolve.

Loosen all tension and feel your body filled with a new energy, a golden energy that flows through your spine and down into your hands.

Feel your hands radiate with Golden Light.

Breathe in again and see the light come into your heart. Feel the great love waiting for you there.

Love yourself and all that you have gone through.

Let this love circulate through your lungs, liver and kidneys. See the smile grow throughout your body.

Let this feeling move into your stomach. See it release any discomfort and fear that may be held there.

See a circle of light spiral through your digestive system and into your lower back. Breathe deeply as it moves to the base of your spine.

See the golden light move down through your legs, through your thighs and knees, into your calves and down into your feet. Take a moment to feel great love for your legs and feet and how they have worked to bring you to where you are.

Rest in this beautiful golden light and feel the peace it brings to you.

Sitting quietly and breathing easily, bring the Mary's consciousness into your heart and feel that love coming alive within you. Feel the power of unconditional love. It accepts all of who you are and forgives all of what you might have done when you were in darkness. Feel the deep compassion that love brings to you.

Let this energy expand into every cell of your body. Feel your body being washed with waves of love—a love that heals, renews and restores your heart. This love is so powerful that you cannot contain it.

Send that love out. Let it extend to all your family, your friends, your city, the continent and the world. Let your love circle the world.

Now see it come back to you a million fold! Let that love come into your heart and feel its light filling your whole being. Give thanks to Mother Mary and God and Christ for this great gift of love.

We can use the daily tools of meditation and prayer to reach all the keys to the kingdom of heaven within.

Mother Mary I do pray
That I can find forgiveness
And release any claims
On any hurt and anger that remains.

And may I have the strength to live
With compassion for myself to find
The keys of forgiveness
To bring happiness and peace inside.

Chapter 8

Forgiveness

Jesus said, "Father, forgive them, for they don't know what they are doing."
(Luke 23:34)

Forgiveness becomes our teacher at some point in our lives, and if we live long enough, we will experience many things to forgive. Christ and Mary were both great teachers who practiced and spoke often about forgiveness. Much of the world then was lost in darkness, practicing an eye-for-an-eye retribution. So when Christ suggested loving our enemies and turning the other cheek, he was offering a revolutionary teaching for humanity. Even now, 2,000 years later, we find forgiveness one of the hardest lessons to learn.

I wonder how Mother Mary felt when her son was on the cross and heard him say "Forgive them Father, for they know not what they do."

Mary also had to forgive what was done to her son. This call to forgiveness is our call to understand why we must forgive the wrongs we have done and other s have done to us.

One of the hardest things about forgiveness is that we must learn to forgive ourselves so that we may forgive others. We may feel that we have not lived up to what we wished to be. Or we may regret some of our actions and be remorseful about them. Sometimes we blame ourselves far more than we blame others for what did to us. In such cases self-forgiveness is very important.

If we could see an overview of many lifetimes of our existence we may see that karma plays a role in what can happen to hurt us here. Of course, not knowing the whole picture, it is easy to slip into "Why me?" or victim consciousness. The hard thing to see is that when we think like a victim we actually draw more of the same to us.

We never really know how long we have to live here, so it is a good practice to clean the slate and do some conscious forgiveness for ourselves and others. In doing this we become more God-like and less driven by our ego. If we ask Christ or God for forgiveness, we may feel the grace of compassion come to lighten the load of anger and disappointment.

A deeper metaphysical look at forgiveness would include understanding in truth we are all one. That we are only separate in this physical form but we are all part of God's one Life.

We all play different roles to learn from in this life. Some younger souls have no idea of the kind of damage harmful acts can do. It is not until you have a higher perspective or a Scrooge like revelation that you can see what harm you can inflict on others and thus yourself.

Read some of these poems on forgiveness. You may be inspired to meditate or pray to find a way to forgive yourself for any hurt you have caused and to forgive anyone who has hurt you. Many blessings come with forgiveness.

Here is a forgiveness exercise to do.

Exercise For Forgiveness

Take some very deep clearing breaths
Go deep within and feel anything that may not be clear within the depths of your heart and soul.
Call upon Mother Mary to be with you.
Know you are safe and surrounded by her and the angels who work with her.
She holds a sacred chalice. She hands the sacred Chalice to you. The chalice can be placed over second chakra naval center.
Move your awareness to the pelvis area and let any old feeling of anger or hurt that are dwelling there come up.
Place you hands crossed facing down over your pelvic area and lower stomach.
Whatever old issues and hurt that may be buried let it come them come out to your hands.
Feel your hands blessing them.
Release any resentment, anger, fear and hurt that you might have been holding on to.

Know you that you can release and let go of those feelings now.
See a clear cut of any threads of attachments those feeling might have had.
Place any of the thing you need to release into Mother Mary's chalice.
Mary now takes the chalice and lifts it up to the higher realms of heaven.

The chalice releases all ancient karma attached to past negative incidents that have happened in this or past lives.
Now the chalice is clear and filled with pure healing waters of purification from the fountain of life.
The pure water of love and light is poured down upon you.
It comes down in waves of pure love and cleanses your entire body, clearing any last traces of past issues away.
Your heart is clear and open. Your body is a pure temple of love and light.
You are now able to forgive your self and any others who may have hurt you or caused harm.
You are free.

Thank God, Christ, Mother Mary and yourself for being willing to release and let go of the past and to begin again with a new outlook and a new life.

A Prayer For Forgiveness

Mother Mary I do pray
That I can find forgiveness
And release any claims
On any hurt and anger that remains.

And may I have the strength to live
With compassion for myself to find
The keys of forgiveness
To bring happiness and peace inside.

For any strife that I incurred,
For anybody I hurt and pain I caused
That I did not observe,
Let me ask for forgiveness now Lord.

I know that we all are one
Though we live in a dream,
And cannot see the illusions that separate us
And we need to awaken to a Higher Reality.

And so I pray to find a way
To forgive all those mistakes I made,
And to forgive any others who I perceive
Who have wounded me in this life too.

Help me to find the key
To the gift of God's mercy that I need,
So I can be released
And by the Grace of Forgiveness be set free.

The Light of the Madonna's Love

In the Holy Light of the Madonna's Love
A radiance shines forth to you,
And softly she reaches out and speaks
These words ring out so true.

Come all ye who are pure of heart
And let your soul be seen,
Come all who seek my refuge here
And I'll provide you sweet sanctuary.

Come all who are broken-hearted,
Come all who have suffered with fear,
Come all who are so weary,
I'll provide you peace in a safe space here.

Cleanse away the past mistakes
With the holy waters from the Source,
Purify your past mistakes and ask to start anew.
Let all of the old ways go
And allow your self to be renewed.

In the Holy Light of the Mother's gaze
There is the power for you to see
What is in the depths of your soul,
With a promise of a better life to be.

There is a Saving Grace here
And She provides you with Her protection,
With a sacred space to pray
To find a Higher Way and She does say,

Come all ye who are in need of comfort,
Come to this holy place,
Where the Lord dwells in His kingdom
And dwells throughout all time and space.

I will provide you comfort,
You will find such great peace,
You will find the love here waiting
And forgiveness will set you free.

Forgive

Deep, so deep is the well of forgiveness,
Deep is the hidden pain and fear.

Trust that the Light of Love calls you
To restore and heal you, so you may regain
The power to serve yourself and others here.

Be attuned to the truth,
And go to the Source and the heart of all.
Offer yourself the option of choosing
To let go of the past so you can be free and clear.

Extend yourself to reach for the olive branch
That the Holy Dove offers you to release your fear,
For there is great peace that is present,
When you forgive yourself and love others everywhere.

You can be free of what is holding you back
From happiness and purpose in your life.
Deep, so deep the well of forgiveness,
So go to the well of love and find what is right.

Go to the well of Love and Forgiveness,
Release yourself from pain and fear,
Pour the waters of healing over you
To find the solution needed for you here.

Lord, Heal This Weary Heart

Lord, heal this tired and weary heart,
Let redemption come to me,
Let the Light you carry
Show me how to be.

All that I have longed for,
Was to know a Love Divine.
All that I've been searching for,
Was to let your presence be with mine.

Here in the sweet hush of dawn,
I try to come to terms with reality,
And the truth is that I'm
Afraid to face the darkness
That keeps me from being free.

Let me make some sense
Of what this world is all about,
Why there is such violence here.
When it's just forgiveness
And acceptance that counts.

I know that there's such glory
In Heaven's sacred land,
Yet here on earth,
It seems that money's the rule,
And power is in command.

Let there be some way for Light
To shine down upon this place,
And see that good is winning,
And we all can see the Way.

May this long, long journey
Be a pilgrimage to peace,
And all of the world's nations
Join as one to find relief.

There is a Song of the Universe

There is a song of the Universe,
There's a song of Life.
There is a song that the heavens sing,
And each song is born of Light.

Listen close to the stillness
And to the sacred sounds,
Hear the music of the spheres,
Sing the secrets so profound.

Each sound holds a color,
Each song is a rainbow that delights,
And radiates forth with an energy
That merges with the One Sacred Sound
Of Creation's Light.

Join together with the choir
Of angels who bring great joy,
Let all who sing their song in harmony
As together we create a Universal Song.

Sing from your heart,
Sing from your soul,
Let your music be heard so clear.
Let it bring forth blessings from on high,
Let it heal and inspire the world.

Every person holds the Song of Life,
Every heart begs heaven above,
For the magic that music brings
Is the greatest gift of God's Great Love.

Bless All of God's Children

Bless all of Gods' children,
Bless them one and all.
Do not judge the way they choose

To live out their time of love.

This world is just a place where we learn,
The world has lessons to teach,
The lessons we learn.

We used to give to the world what it needs,
Bless all of God's children,
Speak to them of love,
Bless all of God's children,
As God in heaven does.

This earth needs more love right now,
And we can learn just how
To live each and every day
With joy and find a way.

To love all of God's children
As we love our own child in such a way,
We can have great compassion
And see into each soul.

Great beauty lies waiting for us to see
And love knows just how,
To be as God and live with love
And share the blessings each day.
So bless all of God's children
And share your love every day.

Forgiveness Prayer

Lord, thank you for teaching me
How to live with your love eternally,
So I can find the way I wish to be,
A refection of your compassion
And your forgiving grace.

Pour you blessings through my soul,
So I can share these words you give,
So I can share through your love
How precious this life really is,

And the great opportunity you give
To live and love and learn each day.

Lord, help me release the negative energy
That comes when I judge others and what they do,
Which sometimes leads me into darkness,
'Til I see how I am judging myself too.

When I can see the light in another's soul,
Then I can find the compassion
I need on this journey,
Until I reach home.

For this planet is such a learning place,
With lessons taught us every day,
It takes remembering that forgiveness is the key,
So we may understand how we can be free
To walk life's path with love as our teacher eternally.

So Lord, let me forgive any
Who I feel have hurt me here,
And let me forgive myself
For any harm I may have caused
By my attitude or fear.

And if we are stubborn
And caught up in our ego or fear,
It may take a little more time
To learn to let kindness be our state of mind.

I thank you, Lord, for the blessings you bring,
I thank you, Lord, for the love you bring.
And whenever I feel need or am in despair,
I know, Lord, that you are always there.

God's Forgiveness

All of the secrets
That live in the shadows,
Bring them out to be free.
Don't let them wallow
In the light of the new day,

They can be taken away.
So let go of them now, here today.

You can be free to smile,
And free to laugh,
Free of the ancient dramas,
And the chains you've
Carried and cursed.

Allow all the burdens you have carried
To be given to God,
And with forgiveness be married.
All of those distractions,
All the crutches you've used,
No longer are needed,
Just say no to them and refuse.

Refuse the negative anger,
So you can enjoy your brief time on Earth.
And let the beauty of the cosmos
Live in your rebirth.

There is a progression that's taking place,
So have faith, my friend, in a better way.
Pray to the Lord,
Raise up your hands
And open the door to a greater Plan.

If you believe the Lord's
Listening right now,
Know that indeed,
He will show you how
To let the shadows flee.
With God's forgiveness, be set free.

Forgiveness Shall Set You Free

On each journey through life,
Through all the struggles and pain,
You travel through shadows and illusions
You have created while on this earth plane.

There is a moment when you need to find
A way to be released,
And you sense the great compassion
That is offered when you finally see.

You are bathed in the healing waters
That cleanse away the pain,
There is a true forgiveness found,
When you realize why to this place you came.

Learn to inhabit forgiveness,
For forgiveness shall set you free,
You embrace that moment when
You can open your heart,
And see that as you forgive yourself,
You can forgive others,
And embrace life's great mysteries.

As you jump into a pool of love,
You see the you in me,
And you understand the road you traveled,
That brought you here and set you free.

You are baptized with gratitude
So love can heal the past,
And all of life's distractions,
And the road that brings you back.

To the truth of this very moment,
And the purpose you now see.
Then you are forgiven,
And with forgiveness you are set free.

The Queen of Heaven

Melt away the walls that you have built from fear
With a breath release all of your worries and cares,
And open up your eyes to see
The Queen of Heaven brings you peace.

She comes in radiant rays of brilliant Light

With a host of angels at her side,
And the love She offers you
Holds the power of healing so divine.

And you can now forgive
The ancient sorrows you once did find,
You are surrounded by the great love of God
And you feel blessings so divine.

Welcome Her Love
And allow your self to be
In Her Holy presence here.

Open your heart and you will find
The healing Presence so Divine,
Open your eyes and see the Vision of Eternity.

And She offers out her hand
And gives you a radiant Globe of Gold,
It holds the Gift of Love
For our fellow man to know.

Take it in your hand,
And let it fill your life
With the Grace of Compassion that grows,
So you can offer this Globe of Gold to the One
And let it's light pour forth to the world.

And see how the power of forgiveness
Is the answer for all and can be found,
And bring it back to a place deep within your heart
And know the grace so profound.

And you are now a part
Of the Love that the Queen of Heaven brings,
And Her protection is there for you to always find,
And there are really no worries or cares
In the soul's perfect Domain.

May You Find Forgiveness

May you find the blessings of forgiveness

That can come and heal your pain.
May you feel the love that can
Restore your broken heart again.

May you find the peace that passeth understanding
That comes when you can see,
That you are here to love and be loved.
And may that peace carry the power
For you to trust in God again and believe.

May you find that sacred space
That removes all doubt and fear,
And may that space bring you back to love,
That energy at the heart of the matter here.

For forgiveness is the key
That can open the door to your heart,
So let go of any anger, hatred and revenge
So you can make a new start.

Ask God to help you find
That forgiveness you need to heal,
And ask for some forgiveness
For yourself so God's Love can be revealed.

May you find the blessings of forgiveness
That can heal the ancient wounds,
May God's Love and forgiveness lead you
To the love that is there in you.

Another Exercise For Forgiveness

If there are energy blocks or emotional blocks in the body they need to be brought to the Light and cleared so that energy can flow through the body without interruption. The body can hold on to fears and hurt and can close down these areas. Negative energy can accumulate around areas of the body and the body can become diseased and can shut down. The most common areas for energy blocks are the heart and lower pelvic areas and back. Emotional baggage can be stored in these areas and more light is needed to clear out these spots.

Once any emotional issues arise practice using the light of forgiveness to help release it. Forgiveness of the self and of others is key to the healing process.

The more you work with Light, issues will arise that need to be cleared so you can be a clear channel. When you recognize that you are one with all Energy it becomes easier to forgive. Hurt and resentment can separate us from others and it can also drain our energy.

Light needs to have the power of unconditional love behind it to work effectively. Doing Light work with others and on yourself takes great courage and compassion. As you learn how to forgive yourself you will find it easier to forgive others.

Life is a learning experience in which we sometimes place challenging situations so we may grow in wisdom and love. With compassion you can see past the problems and look at the soul's intentions. By directing Light to the Soul you can see the bigger picture and you will find it easier to forgive.

When you are doing Light Healing on yourself and find an energy block
Follow these steps:
1. Do deep clearing Breaths
2, Call in the Light
3. Hold your hand on the spot
4. Breath Light into the area for as long as necessary
5. Allow any images or thoughts that come up to be recognized
6. Place emotions and thoughts into an egg-like circle of Light
7. Forgive yourself for holding any pain or anger
8. Forgive any other person involved
9. See Light flooding into the circle and any negativity being released
10. Clear the area in body with deep breaths
11. Give thanks to God and So it Is

Forgiveness can be practiced as often as is necessary. Some blocks have been in place for years and may take a while to clear. If so, make this exercise a regular part of your routine. Believing that you have the strength to forgive comes with your spiritual growth. With true Love all things are possible. Using Light with Love and forgiveness is a life changing tool. You will find it possible to let go of past anger and resentment and replace them with Light and Love and have an open flow of positive energy in your Life.

Be free of all those judgments
That separate and bind,
And hold you to the ego's control
That blocks a Higher Light.

Let true understanding
Shine with love so true,
Then you can see into other's hearts
And know they are doing the best they can do.

Chapter 9

Overcome Judgment With the Power of Goodwill

Judge not, that you be not judged.
(Mathew 7:1)

One of the plagues of our media-influenced society is the tendency to always be judging others for almost anything you can imagine. We hear so many critical things said on TV and radio shows. There are countless publications attacking celebrities for the way they look and what they have done. Without realizing it we judge people by the way they look, what they wear, how much they weigh, and what car they drive.

On social media sites we see how much people want to be accepted and liked. There are so many ways people have learned to manipulate the public to seek to be liked or to try to draw others in to attacking others for what they did or did not do. We are even judged if you don't have a lot of friends or likes on Facebook.

I grew up in Beverly Hills where students were judged for the cars their parents drove, and when they were old enough, the cars they drove. Every outfit worn had to fit in with what was acceptable clothes, that was considered to be what other popular people were wearing.

It seems that things have gotten worse with the social media influence today, there is a very high bar set for students as to what they should wear to be cool. Many more teenagers are being bullied if they don't fit in with the acceptable norm.

When you judge others you are seeing the negative and dark side of them not the Light. This can cause a negative thought to be placed upon them and it can hide their energy. It also causes you to feel separate from them while you put them in a lesser position to you. It is easy to be judgmental about others if you have that attitude about your self. If you have low self esteem you might need to feel others are not gong to think well of you so you may judge them as a protective measure. When you choose to see the positive or Higher Self of the other, you are seeing the good or God in them.

The Soul's Light can have a hard time shining through the multiple layers and walls that the personality can have. But when you use your Soul's Light to See the Soul of the other and the God in them you are following the Path of God and you may then help them to manifest the higher quality in themselves. We most often are looking at the illusion surrounding others and it is easy to reject that illusion and judge it.

If others are doing things that are negative you can use your discerning nature to reject it without having to judge it. Behind every person lost in Illusion is a Soul struggling to learn lessons that will lead them to the Light. When you judge others not only do you hurt them but you are also separating your self from them.

What to Do to Overcome This Tendency to Judge?

- You can be aware of why you judge others.

- Often we judge others to make our self feel superior. This tendency can be based on an inferiority complex. It certainly is a red flag for realizing our ego is in control. Go into meditation and meditate on why your really are judging other's.

- Make a commitment to be aware of any negative things we say about others and realize that any negativity we promote will come back to us. Remember the old saying that when you point a finger at anyone three fingers are pointing back at you.

- Program into your mind that Jesus said, "Judge not, lest you be Judged (Mathew 7:1)

- We can be aware that in truth we are all one. Judgments are usually projections of our own state of mind. If you say something judgmental stop and be aware of what you are saying and see what you might not like about yourself.

- We can do a review at the end of our day and think back about anything negative we might have said about another person and ask for forgiveness for ourselves and the person we may have said harmful things about.

- We can make a commitment to an agent of Goodwill, knowing that Goodwill is God's Will. Negative energy is not carrying goodwill.

- Light by its very nature dispels darkness. We can use our inner Light to see the Light that exists in others. We have a choice on how we perceive ourselves and others. The mind and ego often is in the habit of comparing ourselves to others.

There is an essential Unity in humankind that we disregard when you are acting in Judgment. There is much in are society that reinforces a judgmental nature. I got a very clear message from Mother Mary that this is a very dangerous attitude that our society has, with many dangerous side effects. It makes me wonder how Jesus and Mary would be judged if they were alive in this day and age. Could we even see into the truth of who they were or would they not be deemed acceptable by today's standards?

Overcoming being judgmental is not an easy thing to do if has been in your nature for a while. It might take a daily commitment and practice to learn to overcome judging others. In time you will see a difference.

If you wish to overcome having a judgmental nature you can practice Goodwill. For if you have Goodwill you will not wish to send negative judgmental energy to others. I have included some messages and on the power of Goodwill in this chapter.

A Simple Exercise That Will Help You To Not Judge Yourself and Others

Go into a bathroom or a room with a mirror. Look at your face, gaze deep into your eyes and say, "I love you, you are beautiful." Now see the eyes in the mirror seeing you as beautiful just as you are. Accept the love that you are. Accept that you are a child of God and your reflect God's Love. When you look into your eyes you can see a reflection of God.

Now remember to carry that same attitude with you when you look at other people. See the God in them. See them as an energy field of light. See the energy behind the form.

Here are some Messages I received on judgments and Goodwill.

Beauty

Beauty is in the eyes of the beholder
And beauty is as beauty lives,
There is great beauty in your heart and soul
Let the beauty now be shown.

Who decides what body is beautiful
And what shape is the shape we need to take?
We can love our body as it is
Whatever shape it makes.

We can accept ourselves the way we really are
And realize that our bodies are just bodies,
They will change with time no matter what we do
And plastic surgery only goes so far.

No matter if we age
For in time we all grow old,
And what was once so beautiful to others
Will fade in time just fade and goes.

If we love ourselves we can begin to see
The true beauty that we really hold,
And when we love ourselves
We can really love others too.

No matter how we age
The wisdom with years will grow,
True Love is a thing of Beauty
And It lives inside of you.

Beauty is as Beauty Lives,
So live in Beauty in all you do.
Look deep into the mirror,
Look deep into our eyes,
And free ourselves of all judgment
And remove the masks and disguise.

See your True Soul, you can realize
You are beautiful and you are unique,
You are one of a kind
No matter what others think.

Can't you see the Beauty in you
Is just waiting to be seen?
Tell yourself each night and day
You are beautiful,
Matter what others say.
Look into your heart and soul
And reveal your beauty every day.

Be Free of All Those Judgments

Be free of all those judgments
That separate and bind,
And hold you to the ego's control
That blocks a Higher Light.

Let true understanding
Shine with love so true,
Then you can see into other's hearts
And know they are doing the best they can do.

There are so many lost in illusion
That can not even begin to see,
That there is such need for Goodwill
And the Grace that allows it to be.

If you can understand that God
Has allowed everyone a choice,
To learn all of those lessons they need
'Til they return to heaven and are freed.

And 'round and 'round we go
Spinning on this planet in time and space,
Everyone trying their best
And there's so much to do each day.

Take a moment to remember
That the ego separates and divides,
Instead of each judgment that we make
We could choose to be more loving and kind.

Pray to the God and the Blessed Mother
For the Grace to be,
A better reflection of the Creator
To be blessed by a Higher Energy.

The Fabric of Love

How would you embody this Love
That holds the essence of the source of Life?
How can we judge the way the children of God
Choose to Play here in this field of dreams?

As you watch the Journey that has led us
To the Dance that this Miracle of love brings,
You find the compassion to understand
The depth and breadth of this Creation.

And the power that brings us to this experience
That is beyond words,
Perhaps an echo of the Universe,
Heard in the song of the heart's delight.

And we listen to the sound of the angels voices
That whisper to our souls and encourage us to carry on,
And when we lose our way and fall to our knees and pray.

We offer up our broken hearts to be healed
By the breath of God's Divine Love,
We are swept on the wave of this energy that
Creates the miracle of being.

And we behold this creation dream and the dance of life
That calls us to believe with the innocence of a faith.

Born of such beauty, such glory,
And such exquisite imperfection,

That it cracks open the shell of judgment
And forgives our fears.
And says "yes" to being here,

And we are delivered with the breath of sweet salvation
That holds our saving grace,
And somehow we are redeemed
Once again by God's never-ending Love.

Don't Judge it, Just Love It

So here you are with your life
Now open like a book,
Can you laugh at the human condition
And just Love it and all that it took?

Can you lift it up to the Alter of God
And release it all and set it free,
Can you be objective and let the soul be?

So here you are with the world to serve
And you must find a way not to judge it.
Can you finally find some purpose in life,
And let yourself not be above it?

Can you find the guiding light that's true,
Can you drop the separation
Of you and the world so you can begin again
And find a way to just love it?

We can take this very moment
And say "Yes" to our precious life,
For something in life will guide us
If we get lost in the darkest of nights.

Perhaps it's a friend or an angel
That teaches us today,
Or maybe it's a voice inside of you
For Life is full of miracles
That can set things right.

There is a way in this very moment

That God can be with you it's true,
If you stand in the light of a new day
And take a moment from all you do
And believe in the miracle of this precious life,
And just love it and allow God to love you.

Judge Not

I was asked to perform a wedding
For two women on the beach one day,
And I said "Yes" for I have done so many,
It's inspiring to see the courage they display
When they're so in love
They're not afraid to say it.

The sun was so bright,
The sands so white,
And as I walked to meet them on their wedding day
I heard some visitors I passed by say,
"Isn't it disgusting
That these gay people are getting married?
It's disgraceful what this country is coming to.
How can these people even say they're married
And do what they do in public this way?"

And I then I saw the women standing near
It almost brought me to tears,
These two beautiful women in bridal gowns
White on White, so proud and strong.

They'd heard what was said about them there
But they had overcome their fears,
And had heard this kind of talk before
It didn't matter what others thought.
They were in love,
And so strong in the purpose
Of what they came here for.

One was so fragile
A catheter hanging was in her arm,
She was so very thin
I knew something was very wrong.

Would she even have the strength
To walk to the place on the beach?

And her partner told me
"Yes , we're great,
We've been together for 10 years today,
And this is our way to celebrate
Our anniversary and that we've made
It is almost a miracle
We made it through to this special day.

For the last year my beloved has been very ill
And has spent most of her time in the hospital.
They gave a diagnosis that was so hard to hear
She may not last another year.

And it's always been our dream
To get married on Maui you see,
And we are so very happy
The day has finally come
And we can make that dream a reality."

So they stood there and spoke there vows
And there were tears
As a looked in each other's eyes,
And there was such love and devotion
And such happiness that seem to shine.

When they said the words "I do"
I know that they had made
Their commitment to each other and I knew
That their dream had finally come true.

I wished them well and we embraced
And told them that I would pray
For their life together to be blessed,
With the memories of this day.

And As I walked back from the beach
I heard from that group nearby,
"You know it's sin and God says that it is so
What you do is wrong you know."

And I said for me God is love
And I saw the love that these women have is so true,
I also know that Christ said,
"As you judge others, you will be judged too."
Who are you to say who people can love?
What they do is their business
And I was happy to marry them here today.

And I will always remember these lovely women
In the dream of happiness finally came true,
Wearing their white gowns on the white sandy beach of Maui
They could finally vow their love forever and say "I do".

The Shadow of Judgment

Release all limitations
By letting any negative judgment go.
For judgment casts a shadow of great darkness,
It limits our will to be our Highest Self.

Judgment comes from a place where we negate the positive
And chain ourselves and others
To the patterns that have held us back,
Through actions that are acted out by fear.

With Unconditional Love
And direct understanding of how Love forgives,
We can be free of this darkness and limitations.
And we can free ourselves and be clear

By not judging ourselves,
And by not limiting our own Light and growth.
And thus allowing ourselves to fulfill our true potential.
Whatever our limiting behavior is we can choose to see the Highest Good,

So judge not others, and judge not yourself,
But choose to let God guide you
To a Forgiveness that releases all limiting fears
So you may fulfill your Highest Purpose here.

And to judge not others lest you be judged too.

And we are delivered with the breath of sweet salvation
That holds our saving grace.
And somehow we are redeemed once again.

How Much Good Can You Hold?

How much good can you hold
'Til you let that love that is present
Come deep to the heart of your soul?

'Til the fountain of light
From the chalice of spirit
Pours forth from the Holy Spring,
From that very Source you can know.

How much good can you bring into your life
To share it with others in need,
So we can remove that negative forces
That can bring us down to our knees?

Breathe in the breath of Spirit
And from the essence of Presence we are,
Find a way to life with Goodwill's energy today
And let it fill your emotions and heart.

With kindness set as an intention
And love as our guide on the way,
Let it to lead us and teach us Goodwill
From the center of the core of who we are today.

And we can trust that with our Goodwill
We can find compassion and see,
That Good can be our teacher
And set our judgments free.

How much Good can you hold in your life,
How much of the Good is really there
To fill you with God's Pure Energy?
With the love, Good, we can show we care.

You can feel Good
By doing Good, by being Good,

By believing in the Goodness that you create
And sharing the Good in you
In what you say and do.
In what you say and do.

Live Goodness

And by living and being Goodness
You can express God,
And sharing the living energy of God's Goodness
In your life.

Feel the Joy in the essence of your Spirit,
Let it express through you.
Bring that Joy into your life,
And see how it changes how you feel
And how others feel about you.

Say "Yes" to the Spirit of joy,
Say "Yes" to your life and how you live.
Say "Yes" to the way you live your life,
And what you have to give.

Accept that Goodness that you are,
Accept that God is present.
The Spirit of God is Goodness,
And when you feel the Good
You are a part of Love's essence.

You can enjoy the gift of knowing God,
And bringing that love that God is
Into your experience and actions.
Every breath you breathe
Is a part of God's Great Energy.

For in the Heart of God's Great Love
There is a light that burns like a fuse.
Infuse you heart and soul with energy
And let that light shine bright in you
In all you say and do.

Find The Good

If you truly look for the Good that is there,
Then in your search you will find
God's Love that we share.

The Good that is there in you,
And the Good that is in me,
When it is Good that you seek
You will find it in you, the key.

For in the Good is the Heart of God's Love Divine
And you'll find there a unifying Spirit
That will help you get past your mind.

And it's really as simple as that, my friend
Look for the good
And it will help you to see
The whole picture of life and your destiny.

For there is always some Good
That is in you and me,
And if you judge others harshly you know this is true
Then that judgment comes right back to you.

So try to focus on the Good instead,
And look with the heart
And not with the head.

There is such Good to find
At work in the world,
And it all is a mirror to see
The work of the Lord.

So focus on the Good and the true
And let God's goodness
Come and bless you.

Every Act of Goodwill

To all the children of God
Let Love lead you on the way.
So many times of trial
Have come to you today.

Yet always there is the Light,
To guide you on you to a brighter day.
Always there is the Spirit of God
To call upon when you Pray.

The world needs every Prayer now,
The World needs all the Love you can spare.
Hold the world in the Highest Light,
And Hold out hope for the Master's Plan here.

Every single prayer, every act of Goodwill,
Each and every helping hand,
Can help us fulfill our Purpose
And help all save this sacred land.

Help build the foundation,
For a new and better day,
To help humankind join as One,
It's time to find the Way.

With the Grace of God,
We can work together and find,
The One Love within that Joins us all,
So we can leave the mistakes of the past and broken path behind.

The One Love within each nation,
The One Light of God in all,
The One Peace that heals the ones at war,
And the Amazing Grace that hears the call.

To all the children of God it is now time
To let Love lead you on the way.

Find it in your heart and soul.
To help serve all humankind.

Imagine Goodwill

Imagine a world where we all work as one
Working together for the Good of all,
Yes, it already has begun.

There are seeds have been planted
And the blossoms have been seen,
You can almost breathe the fragrance
Of the brother and sisterhood who hold the dream.

Imagine a world where we serve
The positive energy of Goodwill,
And we let that energy motivate us
And we use it everyday.

When see the Good in others
We can see the God in all,
And monitor our thoughts
To block the negativity's call

And the Light of the soul can guide us
And we set our intentions every day,
To work with love and understanding
And let kindness be our way.

For Goodwill is God's will
And with it there are countless blessings that exist,
For as we bless others
We find what God's love really is.

Imagine a world where Good lives
And with it we have the secret key,
For Good will holds the answer
To bring us Understanding and Peace.

Good Will is God's Will

It is with the Understanding of the Will of God
That we can release strife,
And with Loving Forgiveness find peace
And so let go of our Ego
To find the Power to Believe.

That there is a greater purpose that we are one with,
That there is true strength expressed
In a loving understanding of all of life's roles,
That have played a part in the world's dream.

There is a common spirit living
Within each soul,
That spirit is alive in each grain of sand,
Every breeze, each drop of water,
And every breath to know.

And the Fire of an Eternal Song
Resonates with heart's light
And celebrates the Sound of Life,
Feel the One Light of Spirit alive in all,
Feel the Love that brings us the power to believe.
For as each life fulfills its true destiny

We are all given hope,
We are all drawn a step closer on the path to our common goal
For the Goodwill of all for humankind.
For as we find Good in ourselves and so see God in others
And as we see God in others so may we understand a Love
That brings us together as one.

And the Highest Dream of God's Plan becomes a reality,
And the One Light of Peace is found on earth,
And with the greatest Love, God's Will, lives
In the Good Will of all for humankind.

Practice Following These Steps to Overcome a Judgmental Nature

Go into a state of meditation.
Do deep, clearing breaths.
Go to the Soul and call on the Objective Observer.
Place a person you have judged, in the Light.
See their soul's qualities
Notice how it is possible to observe without judging.
Recognize the unity and oneness of all.
Send the person light and loving compassion.
Send forgiveness and loving compassion to yourself.
Say "Thank you, God."

When you are in the Light of Love you feel good or God towards others. You can experience this feeling of goodness within the meditative state. It takes practice and patience to carry this attitude with you during the day. Learn by choice to bless others not to judge them. You then are sending light not darkness.

There is within every soul
This place of understanding we can know,
A way for us to be able to see
The burdens we carry on this road to be free.

If we could see what's behind other's fate
And stand for a moment in their shoes,
We could find compassion for what they do
And see another point of view.

Chapter 10

Compassion and Understanding

Put on then, as God's chosen ones, holy and beloved, compassionate hearts, kindness, humility, meekness, and patience.-Colossians 3:12

Does not wisdom call? Does not understanding raise her voice?
-Proverbs 8:1

Forgiveness, compassion and understanding all go hand in hand. You could add to that the gift of Grace. For in a sense if you truly understand, you will find a way to forgive and have compassion. If you truly understand, you will see the reason everything happens. When you are ready, you can perceive the role of karma, the reasons you went through any difficult situations and what lessons you had to learn from the experience.

The Holy Mother is known for Her compassion. The masters Buddha and Kwan Yin are also known for teaching compassion.

Compassion is understanding the predicament of dealing with existing with form and matter combined here on earth. As we go though many lifetimes of learning, we experience more compassion for others now going through similar experiences. Some here are new souls in existence, while others have been here dozens of times. Then there are those who are Masters who have chosen to come from a higher realm to help those in need here on Earth. If you experience enlightenment of Christ

141

Consciousness you will have the understanding the Masters have.

It is very easy to see why compassion is such a big key for spiritual development When you see the state of the world from a higher point of view it's very hard not to find some compassion for the people of the world.

It is also so important to understand that we are living in a world of illusion and it is easy to get caught up in the dramas and games played by so many here.

If we truly understand the predicament of each soul as Mother Mary and Jesus do, you will find the need for great compassion.

For in spirit we are all one. Part of the same Father/Mother, part of the Creator's creation.

Part of the problem we encounter in life is the reactionary nature of our egos. The ego would have us believe we are special, and in truth you are. As are all of God's children. All just at different levels of understanding.

For those who come onto this earth plane knowing this it can be difficult because there are so many who do not understand that you can feel very much outside the general state of accepted way of being.

This is the case with many who are here today but it is still not near the majority. So some aware beings try to proclaim what they understand as truth. Others just try to live with love and understanding practicing the principles of good will and harmlessness the best they can

If we have gotten over some of the obstacles other are experiencing it may be tempting to feel superior and to think we are better. A judgmental attitude is just the ego stepping in to separate us from others.

It can be very difficult to walk on the path of the Masters and still be in this world but not of it. So we can call on your teachers, angels and guides.

I have found by meditating and praying daily and calling upon your teachers and guides you can connect with Spirit and your soul will be there to guide you on.

Since I have been calling on Mother Mary as a guide and teacher I have had much more patience, understanding and compassion. The Holy Mother can help to give you such gentle reminders and way to live that works and brings you the light and love you need to serve God.

There are meditative visualizations you can do to give you a more objective perspective on life. One way is to learn use the perspective of the objective observer. If we can learn to step back from our reactions and emotions and see with the eyes of the Objective Observer we can begin to understand with the light and love of the soul.

One day we might even be able to see others through God's eyes.

To stand under the Light you must be open and willing to receive.

To understand is to really get it. This can mean surrendering a point of view to see something clearly from another perspective. You can spend a lifetime learning to understand yourself.

Once you see yourself clearly then you can begin to understand why you are as you are. If you understand your self it is easier to have compassion for others. To understand God you must be willing to be open and give up your own point of view to experience a universal overview. You can then experience the ultimate Light born of Love.

Imagine understanding a pure unconditional love that comprehends all of life. Understanding fulfills the heart's longing to love and to be loved, because it is the basis of love. When you truly understand another you can accept and love their very soul. When you love yourself you understand who you are and accept the path to self discovery. When you experience the Light of your Soul you are able to open the door to understanding . This entails being very open to receiving information and saying yes to it. Yes, I get it, yes I understand now.

With understanding comes wisdom, love and forgiveness. To practice going to the Light and being in the light of understanding follow these steps.

- Go into meditation
- Do deep clearing breaths
- Go to the soul
- Open the heart and be ready to receive
- Ask for understanding of a situation
- How could this situation be resolved with love and understanding
- Be still and wait for answer
- Write down what comes to you
- Comprehend the understanding and register it
- Experience how that makes you feel
- Thank God

You can ask for understanding of yourself, another or of a situation. You must be able to be open and detached to receive a clear answer and a different perspective. You may experience unconditional love when you truly understand. Understanding is a reason to love and gives love reason. It frees you to be aligned with the light of the universe. It is the AH HA of knowing the soul. Practice living in the light of understanding and understand how to love the path of Light

Be Transformed By Understanding

Be Transformed by understanding
The gift that the Holy Mother brings,
For life is truly a miracle
With the God's power of love that heals.

Her grace is alive and waiting
As a blessing for you to find,
Each breath holds the power of giving life
With a love that is waiting inside.

Breathe in this breath of love
This Spirit is alive in you,
Feel the living light of God
And the love which is so true.

Feel spirit and form merging
Tap into that power to be,
Transformed by the Holy Mother
And Her magnificent energy.

Open up your heart and soul,
Open up your mind,
Let your body receive the healing
That is from such Love Divine.

You are a living force of energy
That can bless and serve the Lord,
You can be transformed by the miracle
And your greater purpose He adores.

You can understand
The holy gift of compassion for all,
The Holy Mother is there to help us
She can open up heaven's doors.

And she has brought us miracles
And she holds out her hand,
We can reach and take it
And let her guide us to understand.

Ask for her Holy Guidance
And allow Her presence to come,
She is the Queen of Angels
And blesses us always with Her Love.

Compassion and Forgiveness

Father, Mother God,
And all the Angels of the Light
Help us to feel compassion and forgiveness,
So may see that it's all right.

Let us understand the One
Who knows what's in our souls,
For in that understanding
There is the key for us to hold.

And with that key there is the power
To unlock what's in our heart of hearts,
For waiting there within us
Is the Love we need to make a brand new start.

Father, Son and Holy Spirit
Lead us to the Light within,
So that we can see if we may
How to begin our lives again.

Let the angels protect us
Each and every day
We call upon the Grace of God
To guide us on our way.

Understanding and Compassion

Sometimes I wonder
How it's possible to be
Loved by God and the Mother
So completely, so compassionately.

And if I am loved with
Such understanding that I feel,
Shouldn't I return
That "love others" as do they for free?

Sometimes I don't feel worthy you see
Of such a great love,
And I know that he understands
This too for me.

I feel that I should really do more good
And give back to others
The way that He would do,

How can I ever repay
Those gifts that are given so freely
May I find a way to give to others
A little more each day.

Perhaps all God's children
Are watched over with love,
But there seems to be so many
That are lost in the darkness
That they don't seem to see
The Light trying to free them.

All we can do is give them love
And pray to have the compassion
To realize we'll all get there eventually.
Until that day
We all have so much to learn
'Till we graduate and are able to see
God's Love is given unconditionally.

Because we are all His children
We are all Made of His love.
And one day we will be able
To be given the keys to the Kingdom,
And bring to Earth more kindness form heaven above.

The Path to Understand God's Love

All of your life is a path to understand God's love.
You can choose to learn from it and love it,
So that you can love yourself as God loves you.

For you are the beloved of God,
And you are worthy of this love.
As you accept this truth,
You bring this love into your life.

And you can be of service
By sharing the love God has for all his children,
Without judgment, without limitations.

Just love others as God loves you,
Just love yourself as God loves you,
Just love all life as God loves you.

To do this you must forgive yourself,
And forgive any others you have felt
Have done you wrong and caused you pain.

For when you accept that you are worthy of God's love,
You can put aside the ego,
And the way it separates you,
By feeling you are better than others.

The ego does not let you believe
In your true worth and ways to be of service.
It has played a role that no longer
Serves your Highest Purpose.

For you are more than your ego,
So much more than you may know,
And you no longer need to hide
From who you are, or be afraid to show.

For all of your life is part of the path
To understanding the power of God's Love.
Embrace being under the base standing
Here on earth and reaching for heaven above.

Compassion

Here in the world of dreams
It is so easy get lost
In the veils of illusions that we create,
The trials that come from holding the sacred cross.

This world holds such heavy energy
And there are so many trying hard to succeed,
And to really bring a little Heaven to earth
May take great compassion it seems.

For there are so many seeking
Who are lost in time and space,
And there are those who are angered
By what we must forsake.

So stop and take the time to pray
And ask the Holy Mother's help,
And ask for some compassion
For those who are suffering everyday.

Yes, we need to have compassion
And we need to find a better way,
To stop the ego from controlling us
When we think we are better in this time and space.

So ask for a little compassion
It's a gift that the Holy Mother brings,
And with compassion come the power to understand
That we are one in spirit with everything.

There is such grace in giving
That energy that heaven shares,
It shows us a way to forgive and release
Our judgments so we can truly care.

All is Revealed

In the Light of the new day
All that you are is revealed.
Nothing is hidden.
All is brought forth

To be offered to the fire that feeds
The spark of the soul.
From the depths of the shadows,
The secrets are seen,

All the kindness, all the cruelty,
All the love and the hate is known.
All is revealed in the Light of the new day
To be naked and cast before God to be freed.

The dreamers awake to remember their journey
And all they did to get them through the night.
To see their life as an offering,
Grains of sand that have poured through the hourglass of time.

This moment holds the Amazing Grace of understanding,
That allows you to accept all that you are.
May the Eternal Flame of the Soul
Burn with the Fire of Compassion that continues to let you grow.

May the rewards of the long journey
Bring you to find Love as your true home,
Accepting your life, and accepting what you have learned.
Nothing hidden and all revealed,
With the Love you have given,
Equal to the Love you have received.

Place of Understanding

There is within every soul
This place of understanding we can know,
A way for us to be able to see
The burdens we carry on this road to be free.

If we could see what's behind other's fate
And stand for a moment in their shoes,
We could find compassion for what they do
And see another point of view.

There are so many different ways we live,
So many different ways we dream,
That lead us to learn what we think we need
All will carry us to our destiny.

Understand that here on earth
We all have egos that want to be in control,
To be recognized and applauded and known
So many want just to be loved so.

But beneath the outer shell we see
There is this inner core,
There is a heart that needs to be
Recognized for who it is and what it believes.

Understand we all have needs
Most of the time they can't be seen,
It takes a lot of time it seems
To get to live out our life's true dreams.

And so when we see the bigger picture
And how we have to live together here,
And how it helps see others and care
To look into their hearts and their hidden fears.

So take some time in your busy day
To show some kindness today,
If you try you can find a way
And what a difference that might make.

You'll find a connection to other's lives
That helps us to understand their plights,
With a little compassion for the human race
We can find a place for more love in our life.

Some Gift of Understanding

Here is an offering I make,
Some gift of understanding,
As I greet this day
I pray that I may be truly present and aware
To all that may somehow appear.

With each encounter there is a prayer
To be open to God's Love,
With great compassion for all
In this time and space while here.

God, may Your Life embody my Love.
Let Your Breath fill me with the sweet energy of Spirit above,
So I embody your miracle of being alive,
That allows me to feel that
I am a joyful vehicle for Your Love and Light.

May my heart be open to the emotions
That receive the Joy of life,
So I may embrace the true beauty of Creation
A blossom that flowers with colors so bright.

Bring me the compassion that carries true understanding,
For each who dwell here in form
Would like to experience some form of happiness
And some reason to be born.

Let the faith I have in You
Be the same faith I have in me.
For I know God is with me in all I do,
May I be grateful for Life.

And when I open my arms to the heavens
May the Spirit come through me to earth.
And may I truly welcome
This precious moment into my heart's rebirth.

So I may greet the I am that I am
With some gift of understanding
Some compassion of the greater plan.

The Heart of Understanding

Come, oh come, to this world
And know, the Heart of understanding.
Bring the compassion it takes to be alive
To understand that here God's love abides,
In the Heart of Understanding.

This is not a religion, or a Sunday kind of thing,
It's being here 24 / 7 and all that means
To being human and the truth that brings.

Come, oh come, to the hidden places only you can reveal.
For there is a lifeline you were given at birth
That connects you here with your true worth.

The human heart's so hard to know,
And so we are given the eyes of the soul.
And with that vision we can see the light
That's alive and guides you as you go,
To the heart of understanding.

Take the breath that integrates
The God in you and all you create.
And let that breath bring you a way to be
The love that lives in you and me,
A love that can forgive and set you free.

The power of compassion is what we need,
To live in this world and all it brings,
To still believe in everything that
Leads us to the Heart of Understanding.

The Sweet Smile of Understanding

The Sweet Smile of Understanding brings a Peace
That allows our completion
Amidst the happening of all of life's dramas,

We can get through all that is upon us.

Alive in the Light of the Soul
Alive in the Life Preserver we have been thrown,
A fragile being out there in the stormy seas
And in the drama of the dream we can be
The audience or the players on the stage we see.

We are all in this together
So we can smile and recognize,
The One energy that allows the smile
That brings our wake-up call,

The understanding, and the peace
Which allows everything to be all right between
The darkness and the light that has brought us to see,
A mysterious Presence is a part
Of the Love that can set us free.

The love that waits in our hearts can complete us
And awaken us with a sigh of relief,
And our breath is captured and released;
Our heart is opened and our soul revealed,
And the sweet smile of understanding brings us peace.

I Am One

I am one
With the sound of light,
This symphony that resounds in life.

I am one
With each breath of the gift,
The miracle of the blessings that this life gives.

I am one
With the rising sun
And the source of all the light,
That feeds the Mother Earth and comes,

To bring us this day

And the beauty displayed,
To remind us that we
Are all reflections of the One.

Yes, I am one with the Divine
And all It's mysteries we find,
The dreams in which we dwell
And the great awakening from It's spell

I am that moment of the eternal now
That seems to always be present somehow,
With us in spirit
'Til when we behold
The I am that I am,
This completeness to know.

I am one
With this life,
This eternal fire
Fed by the grace
Of love's holy choir.

And when I feel that
I am alone,
Let me remember the truth
That we are all one.

The Objective Observer

The soul level of consciousness carries the spirit of your being. It also carries the higher level of the mind's awareness. This awareness within the higher self is called the Objective Observer.

The Objective Observer does not get used by most people in their regular daily routine. The Objective Observer is a faculty of your higher consciousness. It has the power to see life from a higher perspective without the emotional and egoic attachments that can effect your point of view.

The Objective Observer can be used to give you a more insightful understanding of a challenging situation in your life. There is not a vested interest in the personality position as much as the soul's interest in how you can use the situation for wisdom and growth. When the personality has an interest in protecting itself it can be very defensive and reactionary.

The true nature of a situation is not often seen and understood. When you involve the Objective Observer you can find out why a situation has occurred and you can see what there is to learn from it. You can also see how to more effectively resolve a situation so it does not cause any negativity. The Objective Observer can teach you much about yourself. You can learn to call upon the Objective Observer so that light may be shed on your life. The lower mind must be taught to step aside so that the higher mind can be functioning in your life. When you are in a state of meditation the higher mind can have a safe place to be. Practice these steps to work with the Objective Observer.

1. Do deep breaths to clear the mind
2. Go into meditation
3. Go to the soul
4. Call upon the Objective Observer
5. Leave an open space to listen from
6. Put a situation in the Light
7. Allow yourself to see it from the Objective Observer perspective
8. Now try to imagine what it would look like through God's Eyes.
9. Write down anything that may come
10. Thank the Objective Observer and God

If you are open to receive guidance from the Objective Observer you can learn to use it as a friend and coach. You can learn to look at your life from your soul's perspective. This can allow you to see very clearly in the light.

The Objective Observer has the power to discern without judging. It can teach you to love unconditionally. It can help you to learn compassion and understanding. It can also help you overcome negative habit patterns and addictive patterns.

When you learn to use the Objective Observer you will develop a positive relationship with your higher self. Learn to call upon the Objective Observer and allow this part of your soul to be integrated into your life. Your consciousness will be brought to a higher light and you will have greater understanding and compassion that will benefit you throughout your life.

This moment holds the Amazing Grace of understanding,
That allows you to accept all that you are.
May the Eternal Flame of the Soul
Burn with the Fire of Compassion that continues to let you grow.

May the rewards of the long journey
Bring you to find Love as your true home,
Accepting your life, and accepting what you have learned.
Nothing hidden and all revealed,
With the Love you have given,
Equal to the Love you have received.

Chapter 11

Redemption

If anyone is in Christ , he is a new creation;
The old is gone, the new has come!
(2 Corinthians 5:17)

What is redemption and what does it mean to you?
There is a process that you will find in this entire book that has to do with
clearing away any past negative habits and any harmful tendencies that we
might have. It can be a long process to clear away anything that we do not
need in our life. It can entail being able to be objective and detached to do
this. It is also very beneficial to our happiness and the good we can do in
the world as we undergo that process.

We read a lot about redemption and the need for it. Often Christians
tend to use it as a threat of sorts. BE REDEEMED NOW OR ELSE, with
the consequences being you burning in hell if you don't listen and change.

My understanding from a mystical and direct communication with Mary
and the Master has much more love and understanding and a lot less fear
and judgment. The fear aspect of religion when used to threaten people has
caused much harm, in my opinion. Love is the magnet that attracts people
to Jesus and Mary. This was the greatest gift they gave us.
We can experience a true rebirth when we are on the path to
discipleship. It can happen with the grace of God, it can happen by our
commitment to truly change our lives for the better. It can happen in many

ways. We can experience redemption. We can experience rebirth and it does not have to happen in church or when we are baptized. We can be baptized by the Holy Spirit with the Grace of God's will. This means that we can experience a true rebirth when we are on the path to discipleship.

The Light and Love of God is always present within you. Your soul carries that light as its identity as does all of creation. Yet as you experience your lessons here and go through your journey in life you can get lost and not see the path of light and love.

As you search for the way you again look for the path yet you can feel separate from your inner connection to your soul and God. This sense of separation can lead you to explore paths that make you realize you do need the grace of God and that light that allows you to see the truth and free you from illusion. Even though you may feel separate from God this is an illusion. For God is omnipresent and you will be led back to the light if you are sincere and ask to be lead to it. The Holy Mother can lead you back to God who is always there waiting for you.

You can find the light of redemption when you can forgive yourself for whatever caused you to go astray and for whatever made you believe you were separate from God. You can begin again on the path with no beginning or end. You may find that your strength to find the way comes from Christ, Mary or others holy Masters. You always can find a helping hand and ask to guidance to help you stay on the path of light.

There are many who have a hard time accepting the word sin or sinners as a judgmental and very derogatory word. According to Theopedia, there are 6 different nouns and 3 verbs for sin. It has been said that it can be translated as to being contrary to God's nature. In Aramaic it can be translated as missing the mark. In Latin it can be understood as guilty.

Whichever way you choose to use the word sin, there can be ways to learn to not be against God or God's will. Not to cherish animosity or going towards the translation for Satan, " Satam" which can mean to hate, to oppose God.

It is as if, you as a Child of God, had lost your way. You can make amends and ask to be attuned to God's will to work with the Good in life. Once you do recognize that we do often miss "miss the mark" we can make amends and try to be closer to God's path. We can forgive and be forgiven and be welcomed home again. You can feel renewed and reborn in the welcome relief that you're are surrounded by light and love always. .Mother

Mary helps save many lives with miracles each day, yet if you are not ready to change then you might not be ready to see the true light of God.

The path of life is long, and it is easy to get lost on the way. If you have faith it will help you to remember your way back home. Sometimes the process of getting lost is even an important and valuable lesson and one that only strengthens you when you do get back on track.

I have gotten many messages from God and Mother Mary about redemption and rebirth. Most all are inspiring and celebrate this as our true gift on the path of the Christ and Mother Mary,

For it is our true self we are coming back to experience. It is the awakening of who we truly are that was shown to us by Christ and his rebirth. Redemption comes in accepting the Love that you truly are

Coming Back

It's such a long, long journey
Coming back to you,
I seek a refuge
I wish to renew.

The love that's there
Deep you're heart,
I wish once again to be a part
Of the grace that saves
And can redeem
With The blessings of the service
I promise to you offer to thee.

I remember the vows
To do whatever I could,
I wish to be redeemed now
To return again to do whatever I should
That can free me to do some good.

I finally have paid all of my dues
And I know the price I paid
Will lead me back to you.

Please come Holy Spirit
Come now to my heart,
Help me once again to do my part,

Allow me to feel that divine love
That only you can impart.

I have such great faith
That the Holy Mother is there
To hold me in her arms,
I feel she truly understands and cares.

And there is such a light
That shines in God's eyes,
I pray for strength and compassion to find.

To you I pray for mercy and forgiveness
For all others did to me too,
And what I had to do to get back to you.

And the journey on that long path home
To find redemption it seems,
To the Queen of Angels
Is waiting there for me.

On heaven's throne I can finally see
All the blessings that have been given
So freely to me.

I accept the love
And I know it's time
To carry on the journey,
To redemption and find that peace
That is waiting there inside.

Believe Again

Gather the bitter disappointments
And the ancient hurts of the heart,
Heal the broken wings of the earth bound angels
Who have forgotten what they came for.

With help of Mary and the lord
We all can accept a Higher Reality,
And if we have the faith to believe
We can be redeemed.

Gather the sad reality
Of the earth's misdirected illusions,
And set the lifeless dreams free,
And help us Mary believe again,
And help us Mary to believe agin.

Long have you tried to protect your heart,
Long has the doorway to true Love been closed.
And yet, once again Mary calls you
To find the path home.

If you can but try to love life
With the sweet unconditional love
That God allows each soul,
Then you can forgive yourself
So that you can believe again and be made whole.

Believe in the power of redemption,
Believe in the amazing grace
Of the Holy Spirit, to bring you to
The acceptance of God's Love in all souls.

The Queen of Angels reaches out,
And all of the prayers of the world
Aid in the salvation that God's Love brings.

So hold on to the power to believe,
Hold on to the power of love,
Release the pain and suffering of the world.
And hold the vision for a transition to a new way.

With the help of Mary and the Lord
We all can be able to accept a Higher Reality
And believe we can be redeemed.

Before the Throne of God

And as you appear before the Throne of God
And the source of Love and Light,
How would you express your Presence in me?

Can you listen to hear,
And so receive true understanding,
Can you receive the touch of Mary?
Reach your hand out and she'll be there,

Feel the angels' wings as they surround your soul,
Receive the grace of the blessings
In your life that come to you to know.
Breathe in the fragrance of heaven's garden
As the blossoms of bliss fall from on high

And let Her redeem your heart,
Redeem your soul, and let all judgment go.
For the Presence of the Lord of Love
Accepts all of who you are,
Just believe enough to be open
To let all fear go.

And let Her Presence be with you
As your guiding light,
And stand before the throne of God
As you would stand before your life.

And be ever so grateful for the blessings
That come in oh so many ways,
And be ever worthy of the lessons
That are given to you each day.

And be a part of the exchange of this love
That expresses God's presence so clear,
As you express the Presence to me
So you can be with the Presence here.

Accepting Redemption

Redemption comes in accepting
The Love that is Who you are,
Acceptance of Who you are comes
When you find your soul and your True Nature.

Your True Nature is eternal

And seeks expression in all that you do.
As you can understand this you can
Forgive yourself so you can forgive others too.

As you understand who you are
You can love yourself,
And see that you are worthy of redemption,
You are worthy of Love,
A love that is compassionate and unconditional.

So forgive yourself,
See your self as Love,
And allow that love to be expressed
In what you do and the way that you live.

And know that you are the Love that redeems,
You are the Light that is the beacon
That allows you to see through the illusion of darkness,
And awakens from the long sleep.

You are the Shining Eternal Soul
And It is this Holy Spirit or you
That would choose redemption,
And let the past go and be renewed.

For God's Spirit is alive in you
And It is this Spirit that would choose redemption,
And would choose forgiveness to be free.
You have the Power to be redeemed
Let all the resentment and hatred go,
Align with God's purpose alive in your soul.

When We Come to the Point of Needing Help

Somewhere here is redemption
And the deal that we have made,
A promise that is our save card
To use when we need to escape.

Or perhaps, it comes when what we see

Is brought for us to face,
And we have lost our hope of innocence
And pray for forgiveness to find God's grace.

There's so much we have to do here,
And how we've come to find
The answers to our questions
And what is left is a prayer and an open mind.

How often can we call out,
To bring us to back to the light
How deep to we have to go now
To discover our hearts secrets belong to humankind.

Somewhere in my soul
Is a memory of a promise that was made
It whispers to me to call on redemption
For it's our saving grace.

And all that we have done is then seen
As some dream and the illusions we made
But once we've called our save card
It's so hard to go back to the games we played.

And here in the promise given
Is the light that is so sublime
It's the power of the Redemption
In God's love that restores us just in time.

Redemption's Grace

Redemption is allowing the grace
To forgive yourself and others,
So that The Holy Mother's Love
Can come into your heart
And restore your spirit to believe again.

The Spirit that sees the power to make amends
And give your life the purpose that you came here for.
The purpose that your soul has held in the silence
And holds the promise that you can remember

In the depths of your being that you can recover.

And there is the whisper that speaks to you to
Release the past and redeem
The power of God's Love in your soul.

And when the Light of Amazing Grace comes,
Open your heart and welcome the Love again
That restores you and recognizes who you are.

And with Gratitude choose to let go
Of all the past hurts and fears,
And say "Yes"
To the Amazing Grace of Redemption.

Great Redeemer

Great Redeemer,
Oh, one that holds the Light of God.
Let your Love fill my Heart and Soul.

So I may remember who I am.
So I my redeem my power to believe.
So I may be healed by the truth
That God gave you to hold.

The Gift of redemption is what you offer
And this I gladly receive.
I understand the Power of Who you are
And your unconditional Love for me.

Oh great redeemer,
Allow me to forgive
Those who have caused me Pain and suffering.
And Allow me to forgive myself,
For not seeing that I am worthy of your love.

For I am a Child of God.
And I see that you offer me eternal Life
And the light to guide me on the path of love

And share the Spirit of God that is alive in my Soul

Trans Form Ation

We are all part of God's circle of life,
Living reflections of the one light,
Spirits here in bodies that live for a while
And then return home to another life.

Christ came to be an example
That showed us how we can be,
Transformers of this form and receive
The transforming power of pure energy.

Bodies of matter delivered first
To earth by the Mother's Love,
Then to be able to express
The blessings of life by Spirit's dove.

And we are created from stardust
And we are spinning through space,
And so often we can't remember
The reason we can to this place.

For we are all pure energy
Here in form for a while to express,
The gifts of love's creation we are blessed
With light through infinite mirrors we see.

'Til we find the eternal salvation,
Giving back with our trans form ation,
The form transformed to spirit making
A cycle of God's great creation.

And Christ asked us to believe
We could live eternally
If we have faith we can see,
How with God's Love we can be freed.

Would You Be The Bell That Tolls?

Would you be the bell that tolls
With that calling to become,
A humble servant of the lord
That worships the sacred one.

Who but those who hear the call
Can listen to heavens song?
And carry forth the holy sound
That brings that message to be found.

Holy Chalice of the Mother
Let us hear your heart's sweet song,
Release us from the darkness
And let your blessings from heaven come.

Let us be the bell that tolls
At the breaking of a Sunday morn,
So we may understand the purpose
That brings God's light to guide us on.

Would you open up your heart
For the truest love sweet song,
That's a beacon in the darkness
That leads us to the holy dawn.

Then find that flame that burns away
The illusions of our time,
And find the very heart of love
That clears away our very mind.

Would you be the sacred offering
And sing the words so true?
Would you be the bell that tolls
And calls us to be renewed?

We ask the Holy Mother

To bring us the love we need,
To find the compassion and understanding
That will set this world free.

The song could find the sacred tone
That open up our life to be,
Found in our calling
And exalts us to be set free.

Would you be that calling
Of the bell that tolls so true?
To become a humble servant
Of this Love offered to me and you.

Perfection Imperfections

Slipping through heaven's halls,
Hearing creation's hidden call,
Merging with the imperfection
Of this human predicaments deception.

That shows us all the great reflection
of this earthly human condition,
That never knows all of the world
And its great imperfections.

We are perfect imperfections
Balanced by life and the fine line,
Between what's wrong and what is right
In the human state of mind.

Father-Mother God
Such a perfect imperfection,
And we must choose
What is our right direction.

Breath and form combined,
The earthly and sublime,
Merged by such an unspoken plan
Such a comedy of humankind.

Perfect imperfection
Accepting this as conceptions perception,
Living out our sentence
'Til our journey completes the penance.

There's such a human gap
That drives us to get back,
The need to get it right
And live the best in life.

Perfect imperfection knows
Only this upside down that shows,
Such a strange reflection
Of heavens intervention.

Dear Father-Mother God
We always have such hard odds,
To be or not to be
To fulfill our Divine Destiny.

So we just do our best
As we try to pass life's great test,
To try to make things right
In spite of the human plight.

Perfect imperfection takes
Such acceptance and such grace,
Forgiveness every day
And compassion to find a way.

What can we do but pray
And meditate so we can find,
Home to that place inside
To hear that small voice
That will not be denied.

And we are part of the one great whole
And yet we can't see the bigger picture,
And so we never know
What's just around the bend
And how it will turn out in the end.

'Cept for all these strange clues

That lead us back to you,
Father-Mother God
We have such difficult odds.

We're here for a just short while
And then gone to the other side,
Always bridging this strange gap
Until we accept that deal is our pact.

Perfect imperfection takes
Such love and forgiveness it takes,
To accept just who we are
All such aging stars.

This divine comedy and the masks
We see played out on each funny face,
As we accept this is our act
As our roles the human race,
And all that Perfect imperfection
that finds us wherever we go.

'Til we make it home
And can laugh at how much we've grown,
The bigger picture is then known
For we are a reflection of Father-Mother God Perfection.

Omnipotent

Lord when I don't know
How I'll make it through the day,
Let me just be ok
In trusting in your will,
So I may know
Not knowing is part of the way
And so learn to grow with faith each day.

Allow the grace of your strength
To sustain me with the power of conviction devotion brings,
So I can just show up
And serve in any way, whatever that might mean.

For you are omnipotent

And your spirit lives in everything,
You are with us with every breath
In the conception of every living thing.

Omnipotent in life
And the light of creation we perceive,
Yes, we are part of your great love
That is omnipotent in the life you bring.

I am part of the great unknown,
I am the breath of spirit,
The bliss of each kiss
Uniting us all as one.

Ever present and never shown,
Not knowing and yet known,
Untying the ribbons and bows
Of this gift of life you've sown.

With such precious blessings
Of lessons so we may grow,
Into reflections of the mystery
That mirror the one great soul.

And we participate in this life,
Forgiving the mistakes we make;
Until we're shaped into a vessel you create
The omnipotence of this time and space,
For we are all part of this one human race
Sharing your omnipotence.

There is always freedom of choice on the path of light. You ultimately have the right to choose which way to turn. It is nice to know there is a safety net in the light of redemption. You can practice and understand the process by following these steps.

1. Go into meditation
2. Do deep clearing breaths
3. Ask for guidance to the soul

4. Call in the Light of Christ or Mother Mary
5. Ask for forgiveness and redemption
6. Ask to be guided to the path of light
7. Write down any steps to take that come to you to follow
8. Release yourself to the love and light of God
9. Breathe in the light of redemption and commit yourself to the path of light
10. Thank Mother Mary and God

We always will come to a place at some time and space where we experience redemption. It comes down to choosing the path we will take to get to that point. You can imagine that you are at that point. That you are ready now to find true redemption. It is important to believe that it is always possible to be redeemed. The light and love of God reaches deep into all souls. You can find this truth by looking inside and connecting with that spark of light within. God is always there waiting to guide you home.

Melt away the walls that you have built from fear,
With a breath release all of your worries and cares,
And open up your eyes to see
The Queen of Heaven brings you peace.

She comes in radiant rays of brilliant light
With a host of angels at her side,
And the love she offers you
Holds the power of healing so divine.

Chapter 12

The Queen of Angels

For he will command his angels concerning you to guard you in all your
ways.
Psalm 91:11

Angels

What a Blessing Angels are!!
The Angels are there to help and protect you in everything you do.
And Angels will lead you to heaven. And be there when you arrive
We have many Angels who we can call upon at any time we are in need.
We have Guardian Angels who are with us for a lifetime.

It is good to know you may not always see Angels, but you may feel
their presence. Often they can be felt as a slight breeze, a very soft
shimmering feeling.
It is good to know that they are connected to God, the source of all
energy. Remember it is not difficult to reach the Angels, all you have to do
is call on the Angels, or think of an Angel and then they are there for you.
We can call on the Archangels to be there in all four corners of our
room or house.
You can pick your Angels. I call upon Archangel Michael to be on my
right side, Archangel Gabriel on the left, Archangel Raphael in front of me,
and Archangel Uriel behind. I call upon Mother Mary if I need direct help

and guidance.

Mother Mary is the Queen of Angels. She rules over heaven and helps to direct the energies needed for those in need in the world. Yet so many who call upon Angels don't think of calling on Mother Mary.

In The Realms of Angels

In the realms of Angelic beings the numbers of the ones doing the work of God are legion and the realm is limitless.

The Queen of Angels directs and guides these heavenly beings that have given their existence. It is hard to even imagine how the calls for intercession are directed. There is constant need for those who wish help.

There is also aid and protection of those who work for the good of humankind.

In the realm of Angels all works are done with joy and with great compassion. For there is a clear understanding of each soul's journey. Many souls have called forth lessons to be learned that are needed to be experienced for the growth of the individual and for the good of the world.

So often the Angels watch, and often with loving kindness wait. When they do reach out and touch a life, many times the one being blessed is not even aware of a miracle happening.

The Divine Mother's Love of the Angels is limitless and miraculous. There is a need for those who are receptive on earth to aid in the work of the Angels.

There are also those who are called Earth Angels who have come into the world to help.

There is such a great need for more to help in the work that the Queen of Angels is called to do. That is why now more and more are being called on to aid in helping those in need on the earthly plane.

A call has gone out for those who can hear on the earthly realm to aid in the works of the Queen of Angels. To learn to help and be of support for the ones in need. For the new world that is emerging is at a level where Angels can work with humankind, and indeed humans can merge with angels to do God's work on earth.

Bless the Queen of Angels in the Realm of the Highest.
And allow the Angels to guide you. Allow them to work through you .

And believe in the miracles that they have brought and continue to bring.

For theirs is a true labor of love from the Highest.

Give thanks to the Queen of Angels and all who work on the Angelic realms and receive their blessings.

The Queen of Heaven

Melt away the walls that you have built from fear,
With a breath release all of your worries and cares,
And open up your eyes to see
The Queen of Heaven brings you peace.

She comes in radiant rays of brilliant light
With a host of angels at her side,
And the love she offers you
Holds the power of healing so divine.

And you can now forgive
The ancient sorrows you once did find,
You are surrounded by the great love of God
And you feel blessings so divine.

Welcome Her Love
And allow your self to be
In Her Holy Presence here.

Open your heart and you will find
The healing Presence so Divine
Open your eyes and see the vision of Eternity.

And She offers out her hand
And gives you a radiant globe of gold,
It holds the gift of love
For our fellow man to know.

Take it in your hand
And let it fill your life
With the grace of compassion that grows,
So you can offer this globe of gold to the One

And let it's light pour forth to the world.

And see how the power of forgiveness
Is the answer for all and can be found,
And bring it back to a place deep within your heart
And know the grace so profound.

And you are now a part
Of the Love that the Queen of Heaven brings,
And Her protection is there for you to always find,
And there are really no worries or cares
In the soul's perfect domain.

Call On the Queen and The Angels

How would you call on the Queen of Angels
And the angels, so they could hear
Your heart's sweet song that reaches out to them
For on this journey they are so near.

Believe in yourself enough to receive them
And the love that they do bring
Mother Mary, Michael, Gabriel, Raphael
And the heavenly choir that sings.

For in the realm of Queen of Angels
There is work to protect us if they can,
There is such a need on earth to lead us
So we can fulfill our part of the plan.

For the radiant light they bring
To help us everyday,
So welcome the angels who see over us,
As on this long journey they light the way.

The Angels work hard to serve the Holy Mother and Father
And his children here on earth,
They work in the realm of Spirit
Where there are legions of angels at work.

Call out to the angels who really do watch over you
And listen to the song they sing,
So you can know the love that inspires them
To bring all of their great blessings.

So how do you call on the Angels
When they are already here?
To lead us and protect and guide us on
And help us to overcome our fears.

And one sweet day may come
When we may work with the angels, too,
And maybe when we've finally made it home
We will come back as the angels do.

Give great thanks to the Queen of Angels, the guardian angels,
And the legions of angels helping the Mother,
And know when you call out in times of need,

Though you might not see them
They are there with you to help you on your way.
So give great thanks to all the angels
Who serve you and protect you everyday.

The Angel of The World

Amid all the heavenly hosts
Who come to watch over you,
There is a Holy Presence
That always will see you through.

The Angel of the World
Watches night and day,
This Holy Mothers Presence carries Light
And is there to show the Way.

The Angel of the World
Is the Queen that is so Divine,
Listen and you'll hear

A Song that's yours and mine.

Amid all the ones who journey
And are messengers of God's Love,
There is a Holy Dictate that comes
From up above.

Hold forth the Light
You're given that is True,
Call upon the Love of the Mother and Christ
Who brings this Gift to you.

The Angel of the World
Reflects God's Joyous Love,
Find the peace and blessings
Of the Holy Dove.

Reach out your hand
And be guided on how to be,
The Angel of the World
Will come and set you free.

The Queen of Angels

Oh these gifts from heaven
That the Queen of Angels so sweetly brings,
Blessings from the ones of Light
That whisper softly in a dream.

They bring the sacred music
And stand in silence and watch the way,
And guide the journey onward
And whisper secrets to my soul each day.

Oh these spirit guides and guardians
That last through lifetimes here,
And all the blessed masters
Who wait 'til we're ready and then they appear.

Oh these Heavenly Blessings
That come from somewhere above,

And bring such a grace and mercy
And return me to Mother's love.

I humbly offer my gratitude
For all you bring to my life,
These mystic visions and memories
That lift me to the soul's light.

There are so many ways you reach me
It seems your there whenever I need,
And if I should be low in energy
You lift me up to be renewed and freed.

I am so thankful
For your miracles you bring,
And I can only offer you these humble words
As heartfelt appreciation for these gifts in everything.

She Shall Bring You Angels

And She shall bring you angels
To keep a watch over thee,
If you just open up your heart
You can find God's Power will set you free.

For in the light of the soul
The Grace of Spirit is alive,
And you can feel that Presence
Awaken the love of life.

And She shall bring you angels
And they shall guide the way,
For with the Breath of Light's purpose,
There are miracles occurring everyday.

So turn your life over to be a servant
And let God's will work in you,
And call upon your angels
To bring you the comfort to see you through.

And when you are lost in the wilderness

They will keep a watch over thee,
Just keep the faith and trust in God and The Holy Mother
To give you all you need.

And thank the precious teachers
And the Master of them all,
And be a living example
Of the blessings given when you call.

And She shall bring you angels
And they shall be there to watch over you,
Just call upon the angels
And let their blessings carry you through.

Let The Angels Guide You

Let the angels guide you
And lead you on the way,
Let their precious blessings
Find you heart today.

Open up to feel
The love they bring to you,
Let their spirit be
A guiding light to see you through.

Let the angels guide you
Listen to their song,
The Music of the Heavens
Can sing and lead you on.

In the angels choir
There is a place to be,
Bring the heavenly hosts
Here with you to set you free.

There are angels here on earth,
There are angels who hear your call,
They come to you and cover you,
Their radiant wings surround you,
And never let you fall.

They bring the Presence of the Lord
And open up the way,
For you to speak with angels
And hear their message every day.

Open up your heart
And feel the blessings from above
Let this love light guide you
To Father-Mother God's great Glory and Love.

Agents of The Angels

We can be agents of the angels,
We can bring their blessings to life.
The angels work with the Holy Mother
Of such great love and light.

When you are in need,
They come and stand by you.
And when you need protection,
They smile and see you through.

Give thanks to all the angels,
And the Holy Mother who guides
Those who are here to be of service,
And eternally do abide.

If you're called upon
To lend a helping hand,
You can be a living angel,
And help your fellow man.

You can be an agent
Of the Queen of Angels above,
You can bring their blessings to life
When you work with light and love.

The Breath of The Queen of Angels

There was a pause, as I asked for the Queen of Angels
To come and be with me,
And I listened and felt the Queen of Angel's Breath
Of Holy Love reach into my heart to speak.

And I took a breath of such divinity
And held it tight to bring it here,
And I bathed in that presence
And ever so gently felt the whispers of grace
She did speak into my ear.

For we can cross the realms of light
And we can always hear,
For we are here to help and serve
And we are ever near.

And there was a deep receiving I felt
As Her Holy Presence came to me,
And the dark of night turned to day
And I felt Her take Her leave.

How do you say thank-you
To the Queen of Angels who appears
And comes to you? Call on her,
Accept by saying "Thank-You, Holy Mother,
May I serve You and bless You while I'm here."

Beloved Angels of God

Beloved angels of God
May I feel worthy of your grace,
May I feel the presence of your spirit
And see the oath that I should take.

And when that little voice that's hidden
There within me
Says "Who am I to receive your blessings?
Who am I to be worthy of your grace?"

Let your light shine so very brilliantly
With your help to find the way,
Let me be able to reach out
To find a way to understand.

I wish to serve the master and the beloved Mary
Who has touched my life,
May I feel worthy of the lessons
And bring forth heaven's light.

Beloved angels who serve the Queen of Heaven
Beloved masters and guardians of the way,
Let me be your celebration
By enjoying the beauty of Creation's face.

For who am I but your smile of wisdom,
Who am I but your servant on the way
To glorify your gifts that you send
And share them with delight each day.

Heavenly teachers I'm your student
Let me be humble and still see,
I am worthy of your presence
And God is glorified through me.

I thank-you beloved angels,
I thank the Blessed Mary Presence here,
I ask to remember who I am
For the Zen of heaven's questions
Can overcome illusions to find a plan.

To live with the space of gratitude
And be a true servant of your will here,
I thank you God for your blessings
That so abundantly appear.

Bless The Angels

To the winged ones of God
Who fly to the heart of humankind,
To be the ones who bring us the gift of love
And lead us to the Divine.

To the host of angelic realms
And the Mother Mary they serve from on High,
As they herald the coming of the dawn
And watch over us 'til Light has come.

They exist in Love in the Higher Realms
And Love is the Power that brings us together as one,
Their Love carries the Light to guide us
For the work that is yet to be done.

For the greatest heritage of angels
Is waiting to be revealed,
The angels will protect us
And guide us to let it be.

Sing the praise of these blessed ones
For they do the work of God,
They show the Way through the darkness
And through time they lead us on.

Listen to their guidance
And celebrate their peace,
The angels live in service of God
And in time it will set us free.

We should live in gratitude for the blessings that they bring,
For in truth it's just a small amount we see,
Of how the angels protect us everyday
And help us to fulfill destiny.

Angel Meditation

Put on some soft inspiring music.
Have a Journal handy.

Take a few deep breaths of God's Light and clear your mind of all thoughts.
Breath in deeply letting the breath feed your body, mind and soul.
See that light's power clearing and purifying you. Visualize a Chalice of Gold being held by God and pouring the nectar of love's blessings down upon you.
It renews and energizes you to be in the presence of your soul.
Now imagine yourself flying to heaven.
Feel the angels' wings lift you high above the world.
How does it feel?
What does the angels' songs sound like? Listen to the song of the angels heavenly choir.
Now imagine yourself in a beautiful Garden of Heaven and feel the light of peace and love that is present there. See your self surrounded by angels.

Now call on Mother Mary and God's angels. Michael, Gabriel, Raphael, Uriel, Azreal, and others you might have a connection to.
Call in your guardian angels and any masters you love.
Ask that they come to you now in this very moment.
Be open to their presence. Feel them with you. Feel their love embrace you with understanding and compassion. Be open to receive any love, healing, or messages you might need to hear.

In that perfect stillness feel their love enfolding you, surrounding you, and smiling at you. Feel the wings they have as a shimmering energy and be with them in this holy space.
Ask Mary any question you might need any answer to. Ask her for any help you might need to overcome a problem you might have.
Feel that answer coming to you and know that they are at work in your life for your good.
If one comes, write it down.
Know that when you write down even a word, many more might come.

Now breathe in their love and light that has come into your soul.
Breathe it into your body, mind and heart.
Feel the joy and peace that this has brought you.

Close this session with a big thank-you and gratitude to Mother Mary and the angels who are watching out for you.

And we each have our song to sing,
All a part of the one universal symphony
That is played with the music of the spheres
The sounds of love creations we can hear.
Oh, these glimpses of eternity
That the Father and the Mother bring,
Whispers of the mystical unfurled,
Sounds of the joy that we try to capture here.

Chapter 13
Union with God

But if your whole body is enlightened, and there is no darkened part, it shall
be shining entirely like a lamp giving you light by its flame."
-Luke 11:36

The Experience of Enlightenment

Mary experienced Union with God. It was the divine connection of Spirit
and form which is also known as enlightenment. I believe she was trained
and surrounded by teachers who guided her on this path.

Mother Mary's union with God is referred to in all biblical references,
yet I never have felt there was enough attention given to the importance of
this achievement. She became One with God, He was Her Beloved. What a
wonderful experience this was that changed the world forever. This
experience took absolute faith, and a love that overcame the ego. It was this
absolute Love and commitment to God that we can learn so much from.

I believe that this union with God that Mary experienced can be
experienced by us.

It was experienced by Jesus and he told us that we could achieve this
Christhood that holds the Light of God's Consciousness.

Yet rarely do we find encouragement to experience this union with God, or a Cosmic Consciousness. This was the Light that Paul experienced that transformed him. It has been experienced by many people of all religions.

Buddha experienced a life changing enlightenment under the Bodhi tree when he saw the morning star. Rumi experienced this bliss of Union with God and you can read his writings and see almost all of his words refer to it. Teresa of Avila, Moses, Meher Baba and others throughout time have had this experience and have found it to be life changing.

We can experience it as well. What is important for us to be aware of is that what she experienced we can experience. Yes, we can experience enlightenment. Yes, we can experience Union with God.

The Light of the Highest can come into our Consciousness for a total transformation of our being. The experience has also been called Illumination. This is an experience that brings one to experience Union with God. There is a very bright white light that is associated with this peak experience. The light embraces you and enfolds you to lift you into a higher dimension beyond your self to be one with all. Enlightenment can come unexpectedly and it comes to people of all faiths.

When enlightenment comes it takes the individual out of a limited personnel perspective and brings the Source of Light into your consciousness. You feel like you are leaving your body and you view the world from a Universal perspective. A unity of all is seen as an absolute truth. You understand that life is eternal.

You're various levels of consciousness is brought into alignment and your brought to the highest consciousness of all. You come face to face with God as pure Light and Love.

You have the experience of "Nothingness" and in "no-thing" is seen the seed for everything. The experience is beyond words as it brings you into the Light of Lights and the Love of Loves.

After having an enlightenment experience the soul has a deeper connection with God and there is an understanding of your true purpose which is to serve God and to make it possible for others to see the miracle of Life and Light.

You can experience various levels of this bliss in your meditative state, but there can not be 10 easy steps given to reach enlightenment.

Enlightenment is a gift from God and is achieved when the soul is ready for it.

To achieve enlightenment you must be able to let go of your little self and experience a death of sorts of the personality. It does give one a sense of being reborn. After this experience you see the world in a new light. You may see auras and have a heightened sense or hearing and a new sensing of color.

You sense the power of a single moment in the here and now. You can see the spark of God in everyone. The Masters of Light have gone through this experience and it has been a part of the spiritual unfoldment that we shall have come to us somewhere on our Path of Light.

Mystics throughout time have spoken of Illumination. It can be the culmination of many lifetimes on the path to God. It is life changing and allows you to feel Love in its purest form and Light in all its power and glory. The Ecstasy is memorable. Life, however, in its everyday pattern does continue on after Enlightenment. You just see it in a different Light and with far greater Commitment to serving humankind for the fulfillment of God's Plan.

Mother Mary had this and a higher experience of not only experiencing union with God but also taking on the ultimate experience of bringing forth the highest being who would be able to stay in this enlightened state of awareness and work from that sate to help save humankind.

There are different level of enlightenment and we may not achieve enlightenment in this lifetime. We can plant the seeds of enlightenment and the birth of the Christ within our soul. This is our destiny, this is our path, not for just the goal of enlightenment. For enlightenment is just the beginning of the way we can help serve others after we have seen our higher purpose.

The Heartbeat of The Lord

Listen to your heart
And trust it enough to believe
The words that come
Will guide you on the path on.

Listen to the heartbeat of universe
And let it set your spirit free,
Accept the truth and listen to be

The love of the Divine that lives in everything.

Listen to the guidance that you hear,
Let go of your busy mind
And listen to the heart my dear.

To return to the love
That will guide you on to find
Your purpose and carry on,
Return to the heart and soul
To let that love there grow.

For love is our true answer
You need to believe,
That with this love is the key
To open the door to our true destiny.

So listen to the heartbeat
And the sound of light,
Let that very energy be aligned
With your purpose in life.

Find you can be one with this energy
That holds the very breath of God,
For the Holy Spirit can speak to you so you can be
An instrument of love.

That reflects the music that holds
The truth of God's harmony
And gifts that always come,
When you listen to the heartbeat of Creation
You'll be in tune with the rhythm of love.

The energy universe
And cosmic mysteries that unfold,
The power is waiting there within
Listen to the heartbeat of God's love.

Listen to sound of life,
Listen to each breath
And be attuned to the force
That draws us to the light.

Each and every breath
Holds the energy of our being
That is the gift that lives
In the heart beat that he gives.

And his disciples are attuned to hear
The anchor that is dedicated
To our soul purpose that appears.

Listen to the spirit,
Let that spirit speak
To be a part of God's greater purpose
And the holy energy it reveals.

Listen to the heartbeat
Be in tune with that love,
Let it guide you every day,
Until you become the echo of God's love.

How Sweet

How sweet the divine fragrance
The garden of heaven brings,
How precious the Love that blossoms there
With the grace of God' nurturing.

Breathe in the holy moment
That holds the light of the soul,
Receive the gifts that were promised you
When your spirit took control.

You can come to the garden to worship,
You can sit here in silence and pray,
You can visit with the Masters and the angels
Who guide your way.

How sweet the fragrance of heaven

How great the comfort it can be,
Let the radiance of God's blessings
Bring a Peace that heals and sets you free.

Lay down all your burdens,
And enter here to be revived
With the spirit that dwells inside you,
And feel the love that heals your life.

How sweet the Blessings of the Mother
How grateful I am to be in the Presence
Of God's sweet gifts
That the garden of heaven brings.

Peals of Silver Laughter

Peals of silver laughter
Fall from the stars,
As the Spiral of the Universe spins to the sound
Of a burning spark of Light.

Within the Mind of God the ember burns,
The Light is fed by the Ones
Who hold the torch.

We choose to believe
In the brilliance of the Life
That can be a reflection of the
Sweet song of the cosmos,
And we are molded to the form of our beliefs.

We dare to say "Yes"
To the Divine Dance,
We breathe in the grace
Of the deep bow to Spirit.

And so we allow ourselves to listen,
To laugh along,
To dream,
And to be a sweet vessel of the Love
That knows our Highest Intentions

And our daily way of dealing
With a reality
That is so much more than it might seem.

So let go and dance to the laughter of the dream,
Let the Light dissipate the fear
And hold the chalice of your heart to the stars
To be filled with Eternal Love
With God as your partner and guide.

Behold The Face of God

Behold the face of God
Seen as the One Heart of the human race,
Behold the vision that leads you to see the glory,
The Light God brings to earth.
Bring the love that is alive in the Presence
Here into your heart.

Breathe in the depth of that Love,
Breathe in the healing that comes with that divine love,
Breathe in the Christ's Spirit
And the Power it has to heal the wounds you have felt
So you may become whole again.

Can you feel the Presence of God in your heart and soul?
Can you see the Glory of God's gifts here on earth?
Can you believe that the Christ can set you free?
For here is the miracle of God at work
Through the grace of the ones who carry the Cosmic Cross.

And when you accept this light and love
Into your heart and soul,
Your life becomes one with God's divine purpose
And aligned with the power to fulfill God's divine plan.

For the new day is here and there is great joy!
So let go of all the pain and sorrow

And release the chains of limited thinking.

For now there is more beauty, more light and love,
And all you have to do is believe and it is so.
Believe that it is possible,
Believe in the new reality
And bring it into being.

With great thanks to God
For as you believe so it is.

Glimpses of Eternity

Oh, these glimpses of eternity,
These mirrored reflections
We are given to see,
God's creation we are given to be.

With the glory so beautiful to behold
That come in so many ways that are shown,
And bring such blessings to the soul
With so many infinite mysteries to know.

Oh, these glimpses of eternity
Heard in the song the universe sings,
That opens the door to the heart
With the promise of our eternal rebirth.

How can we compare the offering,
The symbols of these words,
Just particles of God's Holy Life
A shadow of the truth of divine light.

And we each have our song to sing,
All a part of the one universal symphony
That is played with the music of the spheres

The sounds of love creations we can hear.

Oh, these glimpses of eternity
That the Father and the Mother bring,
Whispers of the mystical unfurled,
Sounds of the joy that we try to capture here.

All just part of the one Great Whole,
Pieces of the Universe expressed here to know,
Singers of the Universal Soul
With these glimpses of eternity shown.

Sweet Love of the Lord

Sweet love of the Lord,
Let the spark of light within my soul.
Be ablaze with the eternal fire
That is of your spirit.

May divine love teach me to believe,
In my heart of hearts,
That such a sacred gift you have given me,
That feeds my faith, and nourishes my life,
In this very moment.

When I try and try in my mind
To justify the how's and why's,
And humbly accept that
You are the Way, the Truth and the Life.

May I drink from the sacred chalice of spirit's source,
May I breathe in the life force of redemption,
May I offer what I have to serve
The great I Am that I Am.

As I walk on the path,

And find the blessing here on earth,
I see your love and light,
I pray your true reflection in of my life.

Glorify God

All of life glorifies God,
All of the ways of God's Love
Leads to understanding and respect of all humankind.

We each choose our own path,
And call upon the Mother who is guiding us
To find the answers that she has found.

Many are the paths to God's Light,
And infinite are the ways we can find God's Love
At work in this world
If we look, indeed, we'll find.

And all of the Masters teach us
That our lives are to be one with the Living Light,
To shine with the Love that leads us to see God's Spirit
Living in the soul of every being,
A seed of God's divine garden
That is planted to bring heaven to earth.

See the beauty that was born of the union
Of Spirit and matter as one,
See the smile of great joy that comes
In this miracle of life.

And bless all of God's children
As you bless all of the masters and teachers of God's Love,
Each is seeking their way to love and be loved.

And in the Light of that Love

Shines the gift of God,
And it will take all of the children of God to find
A way to live together to make
This garden of Paradise God created.

Where we all can live in peace in the world
To live with Good Will towards all,
So God's Love and Light can fulfill it's
Purpose and the divine plan for humankind.

Bring the Holy Energy of this pure grace
Into the deepest level of your consciousness,
To join you with the Breath of Spirit
In a union that is your divine destiny.

This is what you have been waiting for,
This is the moment of "Yes",
Let the beloved of God lead you
To this possibility, and believe enough
To give your self to God

So you may serve with the love
That God's blessings bring,
And the Light to lead you through the darkness of night,
Holding the vision of your life's mission fulfilled.

Do not deny your self to God,
Let your heart and soul say "Yes!"
Let your mind and body be transformed,
And the deepest gratitude give great thanks
So it may be.

Holy

Holy, holy , holy,
The power of life pure energy,
As a celebration of God in everything
That radiates forth love's divine song.

The singing of the morning birds,
The beauty of creation's words
That speak in a whispers and teach
The gift of spirit so alive and free.

Holy is the breath of light,
Holy is the blessings so bright,
These infinite sensations that bring
The visions of God's divine creation.

Here we are able to become our dreams
And to bring forth life,
And with grace be redeemed
The divine blueprint that evolves eternally.

Holy, holy, holy,
The power we have to create
A true reflection of heaven's place,
Yet alive here in this time and space.

Recognize the gifts you have
And hear the holy song,
Give thanks for all the blessings that abound,
This life's music and symphony of sounds.

We are miracles that are awakening
To God's highest vibrations echoing,
And evolving, and transforming creations,
Such great wonders of the Mother's making.

Celebrate the gifts you've been given
And in the silence of the soul just listen,
Give thanks for God's love that's alive
This presence so holy in our lives.

Love God With All Your Heart

Love God with all your heart,
Love God with a passion that burns
As the One Flame of All Creation.

For God is the Creator and the fire
That consumes all of the mistakes and illusions,
To leave only the Truth of your Existence,
So that you may finally be free.

To give you freedom from the dreams
That have held you prisoner,
And allowed you to sleep while
Passing time here on earth.

But each breath is a prayer for Life,
Each thought can be set as a direction
In the compass that will guide you Home.

And each moment is a revelation
That unveils the mysteries to be
Answered by the soul's brilliant light
With the power to set you free.

Bring the Light of God's Love into your heart
And let it burn brightly through eternity,
Let it be the presence that awakens you
To the Holy Spirit's many gifts.

For this is the heart's true yearning,
This is the key to the answers promised,
This is the time for the truth to be heard.

This is the awakening of your true nature,
Stripped bare and standing naked and free.
And God is at the heart of it all,
Alive within your soul, right here and now.

God is the fire, the passion and the awakening,
God gives you the freedom to be you
And to find the Truth within yourself,
And the love that will redeem you to eternal life
In the union of the One in all creation.

You Are a Reflection of The Highest

You are a reflection of the light of highest
Brought here to live in this form,
You are the love of the Mother
Here to serve the holy one.

Are you ready to be seen
For who you really are,
Are you ready to reveal the truth
And be a servant of the Lord?

For the seeds have all been planted,
For so long we've watched them grow,
And there are now so very many
Who are ready to be now able to know.

There are those who are here to fulfill
Their true purpose they can show,
And they can work to help guide others
To become in tune with their souls.

It is time to say "Yes"
To the truth of who you are,
It is time to embrace your life
And shine forth the gift of divine light.

There is a new door opening
And now we can be

Open to the opportunities
In the Presence of a Higher Reality.

All of the prayers are unfurled
Across the energy fields of the world,
By the servants of the Lord
To join together as one.

Say "Yes" to the door that is open
And step into a new way of life,
To see the changes that are needed
To become a servant of the Highest Light.

We can experience enlightenment. I'm basing this exercise on an experience that happened to me many years ago.

Go to your place of meditation.
Take in a few deep clearing breaths.

Now go into the place of silence within and allow yourself to connect with your inner self. Ask for the Presence of the Mother to lead you to your soul.

Be with the light of the Soul and let it take control Let go of the hold of your body and mind.

Find the place of the Objective Observer in your soul. The objective observer is that part of you that is not part of the ego, it is a place in your soul.

Now allow the light of the soul to guide you above the body and out over the area where you dwell. Continue on until you are soaring like a bird higher. Just like Google Earth you moving far above the earth. Continue onward and upward to the higher realms of heaven.

The earth now looks so small and so distant. You can not even see where you live.
Continue on until you leave the world behind and move into the highest light and move to the throne of God.

You are enveloped in the most unconditional love you can imagine.
You realize that God and the Mother are there face to face with you.
You see God Eyes and God sees into the soul of your eyes.

Now you see through God's eyes and see yourself as God see you.
You realize the truth of who your are. You are God and God is alive in you.
You merge in love with them as one.

Now it is time to come back to earth knowing the truth of who you are.
You know you must serve this love. As you come back the objective observer carries you gently back into your body.

And within each Atom, within the Presence of being
Within each ray of Light the Prayers are Heard.
The Prayers change your vibration
And open the Channels to Gods Heart.

And as you Pray for Me,
You will be aligned
With the Light of God's Spirit.
And you will Understand how my Beloved Mary
And how the ones of heaven and the Masters Pray.
So Pray for me each and every day

Chapter 14

Prayers

Therefore I tell you, whatever you ask for in prayer, believe that you have received it, and it will be yours. - Matthew 11:24 NIV

There is wonderful comfort and power in prayer. If you encounter a situation that is overwhelming and downright scary, you will find that it helps to take a few moments to go within and pray. Have a conversation with God. Ask for guidance and protection. Don't be afraid to ask for help. God is there for you, and the spark of His light and love are always with you to call on.

Talk to God or Mother Mary as if they were your closest friend. They know the whole of you, more than any other person may. Even if you don't feel it makes a difference you will find that it helps to develop a relationship with them. I find I have a different conversation with Mother Mary than I do with God. It's a little hard to describe but if you're a woman and were at lunch with girlfriends you would feel you could confide in them in a different way than you would with a male friend.

There are many religions that have differing point of view about prayer. Many get extremely upset if you pray to anyone but God. I certainly do think God is the one source of all Creation. I agree that prayers to God are good. I also feel that there is nothing wrong with praying to Mother Mary if She is your Guardian and Guide. She certainly can be one to carry forth the energy for you. Many Christians call her the Mediatrix, which according the Roman Catholic Mariology refers to the intercessory role of Mother Mary as a mediator in redemption by Jesus Christ.

Much about prayers are misunderstood. I have found if you go with an open heart and pray with the right intention and ask for the prayer be sent for the Highest Good of all it takes your personnel ego out of it. We have no idea what really is for the highest good, even though we always want our prayers to come true. It is God's Will that has to be accepted.

It is important to know miracles happen every day, but they do not happen on command. It is ultimately God's Will that is at work in the world, not our will. Prayers do work, but only if they are in the divine higher good for all. We cannot even begin to imagine the bigger picture at work in the path of each soul's journey, only God can know that. I try to end prayers often with "Thank-You God", which seals the belief that you know your prayers were heard.

Prayers are often spoken from the mind when being read. Try speaking prayers from your heart!

See what a difference it makes. Speaking from your heart changes to energy field that the prayers are sent from. It is like having a heart to heart conversation to the one you love. Always remember that you should keep prayers from having negative statements in them The more you say something negative you are reinforcing that negativity.

The prayers here cover a wide variety of religions and philosophies. Some are traditional and some are more spiritual. Find the ones that resonate for you.

The first set of prayers shared here are traditional, mostly from Catholic sites.

I have a collection of prayers I wrote that I share with you in the second section here

Traditional Prayers

The Secret of Mary-St. Louis Marie de Montfort

Come, Holy Spirit Holy Spirit, God of light, From your clear celestial height Your pure

beaming radiance gives

Come, Father-Mother of the poor

Come with treasures which endure

Come, light of all that live

Of all consolers you are best

Visiting the troubled breast

Your refreshing peace bestow In our toil,

Your comfort sweet Pleasant coolness in the heat

Solace in the midst of woe

Light immortal, light divine

Visit these hearts of yours

And our inmost being fill

If you take your grace away

Nothing pure in us will stay

All that is good is turned to ill

Heal our wounds, our strength renew

On our dryness pour your dew

Wash the stain of guilt away

Bend the stubborn heart and will

Melt the frozen, warm the chill

Guide the steps that go astray

On those who evermore, To you, confess

And adore In your sevenfold gifts

Descend Give us comfort when we die

Give us life with you on high

Give us joys which never end. Amen.

The Peace Prayer of St. Francis

Lord, make me an instrument of your peace.
Where there is hatred, let me sow love.
Where there is injury, pardon.
Where there is doubt, faith.
Where there is despair, hope.
Where there is darkness, light.
Where there is sadness, joy.
O Divine Master, grant that I may not so much
Seek to be consoled, as to console,
To be understood, as to understand,
To be loved, as to love.
For it is in giving that we receive.
It is in pardoning that we are pardoned,
And it is in dying that we are born to Eternal Life.

The Hail Mary

Hail Mary, full of grace, the Lord is with thee, blessed art thou amongst women and Blessed is the fruit of thy womb, Jesus. Holy Mary Mother of God, pray for us sinners Now and at the hour of our death. Amen.

According to Alan Hefner

"The initial words, "Hail Mary, full of grace, the Lord is with thee" is the salutation from the Archangel Gabriel as read in the Gospel of Luke, (1:28). These are the words that the Archangel saluted Mary with when he announced to her that she was to give birth to the long awaited messiah. The next portion of the prayer is the salutation that Mary receives from her older cousin Elisabeth when later visiting her, "blessed are you among women, and blessed if the fruit of thy womb." (1:42)

The second part of the prayer, the closing petition, "Holy Mary, Mother of God, pray for us sinners now and at the hour of our death" was "framed by the Church itself" as officially stated by the Catechism of the Council of Trent."

We turn to you for protection, holy Mother of God.
Listen to our prayers and help us in our needs.
Save us from every danger, glorious and blessed Virgin.

From the Catholic online.org this is an ancient prayer to the Virgin Mary

Memorare

Remember, O most gracious Virgin Mary that never was it known that anyone who fled To Your protection, implored Your help, or sought Your intercession was left unaided. Inspired with this confidence, we fly to you, O Virgin of virgins, our Mother. To You we Come; before You we stand, sinful and sorrowful. O Mother of the Word Incarnate, Despise not our petitions, but in Your mercy, hear and answer us. Amen.

Father Claude Bernard, who stated that he learned it from his own father. It first appears as part of a longer 15th-century prayer, "Ad sanctitatis tuae pedes, dulcissima Virgo Maria."

"Let nothing disturb the silence of this moment with you, Oh Lord."
St. Theresa of Avila

"Hail, Mary, full of grace, the Lord is with thee. Blessed art thou among women and blessed is the fruit of thy womb, Jesus. Holy Mary, Mother of God, pray for us, sons and daughters of God, now and at the hour of our victory over sin, disease and death."
Mark Prophet

Mary Undoer of Knots-Pope Francis

Mary Undoer of Knots
Pray for Us
Through your Grace, your intercessions, and your example, deliver us from all evil, Our Lady and untie the knots that prevent us from being united with God, So that we free

From sin and error, may find Him in all things May have our hearts placed in him, and may serve him always, in our brothers and sisters, amen.

Originally inspired by a meditation of Saint Irenaeus (Bishop of Lyon and martyred in 202) based on the parallel made by Saint Paul between Adam and Christ. Saint Irenaeus, in turn, made a comparison between Eve and Mary, saying:

Descent of the Holy Ghost

Jesus, infuse us with the Comforter, the Holy Ghost, enlighten us with the light of Your Spirit, with His strength enter in the deepest parts of our hearts and heal us. Deliver us, Fill up our hearts with Your love. Make us apostles of Yours, dear Lord. Let us ask Mary the gift of true love, the gift of prayer from the heart.
"Come Holy Spirit, come by means of the powerful intercession of the Immaculate Heart Of Mary, Your well-beloved Spouse."

Hail Queen of the Most Holy Rosary my Mother Mary, Hail! At your feet I gratefully Kneel to offer you a Crown of Roses, full blown white roses, tinged with red of the passion, With a glow of yellow light, to remind you of the glories, fruits and sufferings of you and Your Son, each rose recalling to you a holy mystery; each ten bound together with my Petition for a particular grace.
O Holy Queen dispenser of God's graces and Mother of all who invoke you! You cannot Not look upon my gift and fail to see its binding. As you receive my gift, so you will Receive my petition; from your bounty you will give me the favor I so earnestly and Trustingly seek.
I despair of nothing that I ask of you. Show yourself my Mother!

Excerpt from Petition Prayer of 54 day Rosary Novena

The Assumption of The Virgin Mary

Now that Mary is raised into heaven, She prays for Her sons and daughters, those sons And daughters Jesus left Her when He was on the cross. Mary, pray for us, You know Our fears, take us into Your Heart, the Heart of a Mother. Help us now and in the Time of our death to be with You in Heaven. We ask of you a devotion to Your Immaculate Heart, where we may take refuge in times of trouble.

Excerpt from Petition Prayer of 54 day Rosary Novena
Marian Prayer

"Mary, my Mother, I give myself totally to you as your possession and property.
Please make of me, of all that I am and have, whatever most pleases you.
Let me be a fit instrument in your immaculate and merciful hands for bringing
The greatest possible glory to God"

The Serenity Prayer

God, grant me the serenity to accept the things I cannot change,
The courage to change the things I can,
And the wisdom to know the difference.

The Unity Prayer of Protection

The light of God surrounds me,
The love of God enfolds me,
The power of God watches over me.
Wherever I am, God is.
And all is well.

The Lord's Prayer: Traditional Version

Our Father, who art in Heaven,
Hallowed be thy name.
Thy kingdom come,
Thy will be done,
On Earth as it is in Heaven
Give us this day our daily bread,
And forgive us our trespasses,
As we forgive those who trespass against us.
And lead us not into temptation,
But deliver us from evil.
For thine is the kingdom, the power and the glory, forever and ever. Amen

Aramaic Lord's Prayer

The Lord's Prayer (There have been many translations of the Lord's Prayer. Here is
That I love. They are translated form the Aramaic version by Jon Marc Hammer.)

Father–Mother of the cosmos, shimmering light of All,
Focus your light within us as we breathe your holy breath.
Enter the sanctuary of our hearts,
Uniting within us the sacred rays of your power and beauty.
Let your heart's desire unite Heaven and Earth through our sacred union.
Help us fulfill what lies within the circle of our lives today.
Forgive our secret fears, as we freely choose to forgive the secret fears of others.
Let us not enter into forgetfulness, tempted by false appearances.
For from your astonishing fire comes the eternal song
Which sanctifies all, renewed eternally in our lives and throughout creation.
We seal these words in our hearts, committed in trust and faith.

New Age Invocation

From the Point of Light within the Mind of God
Let light stream forth into the minds of humanity.
Let light descend on Earth.

From the point of love within the heart of God,
Let love stream forth into the hearts of humanity.
May the Christ return to Earth.

From the center where the will of God is known,
Let purpose guide the little wills of humanity
The purpose which the Masters know and serve.

From the center which we call the human race
Let the Plan of Love and Light work out.
And may it seal the door where evil dwells.
Let light and love and power restore the Plan on Earth.

Originally written by Alice Bailey who got it from The Tibetan

Prayers I Wrote

Prayers of Praise

When our prayers are turned to Praise
We are celebrating the power of God

At work in our lives
We are recognizing that God works through us
And the ones who serve him as they may

And we stop and give God thanks
For the one who planted the seeds in this fertile field
For these seeds become the flowers
That blossom and grow eternally

And we pray for all those who wonder down this path
And our prayers are sometimes words
And sometimes they are songs
And our prayers are the way we live our lives
With the blessings that have come.

And we celebrate the blessings
And we are here today to say
Thank you for planting the seeds of Love
In our heart and souls so very long ago.

And now we rest in the garden
And inspired by the one who planted those seeds
And we see all of the beauty from the Flowers
That have blossomed to be Blessings of Great beauty
That grow in the garden of light.

So today our prayers are prayers of praise
For those who have led and cared
And we stop and say thank you for the journey and the grace
And our prayers today are prayers of praise

And we say thank you for the many blessings
Of what has brought us here
And our life is a prayer to those who have followed us here.

Your Life is An Answered Prayer

Oh, Great Father of all Light
Oh, Great Mother of Divine Love
We bow before you and give thanks for the Divine mystery
Of our Life and the Sacred way of truth.
We open our hearts o the most powerful

Of Truths that guide us to your revelation.
That our Lives are an Answered Prayer.

We give thanks to the Angels and Servants of the Lord,
Who work to bring the blessings of your being here on Earth.
And to all who Pray,
May you find comfort in the communion you have with God,
The Father and the Son, and the Holy Ghost.
For your life is an answered prayer.

Leave an opening always for miracles to come into being.
And know you are a miracle in being.

Leave an opening to listen and hear the Lord,
And know He is with you always.
Hear the Lord speak to you in the quiet
Spaces between each breath, between the night and day
Between the highest and deepest levels of being.
For your life is an answered prayer.

Leave an opening to bring about changes that can lead
You to find the Way to be with God.
To see with the Eyes that Behold the Glory of God at Work in life.
For your life is an answered Prayer.

And leave a way to express the Gratitude
That comes when you realize your life is an expression
Of how prayers are answered.
Of how God works through us
To fulfill His Purpose and Plan.

For His love and Light hold the Way to be attuned
to the Perfect Energy of God's Blessings Here on Earth,
For your life was an answered Prayer.

Speak to Me Lord

Speak to me, Lord of the Heavens on High,
Let me live with your truth as my guide;
Let me hear Creation's song,
So that I can be able to sing along.

Let my words accompany your theme
And let this be my humble offering.
Let your light shine down on me
So I can focus on what you'd have me see.

And I see the beauty of this creation here,
And I love the music of the spheres I hear,
And this gives me hope on the journey I'm on
To be able to give voice to your sacred song.

May I find the time to be able to serve
And share what comes to me,
And so honor your words
And be able to find my purpose here.

Speak to me, Lord of your Love and the Way,
For I wish to walk your path each day;
I thank you for all the blessings you bring,
I learn so much in this life I lead.

May your light ever shine
So we all can see
The power of the Love that is
The greatest gift in this life that we live.

Prayer for Protection

Beloved heavenly Father and Mother
Who are in heaven as on earth,
Beloved Angels and Masters
Queen of Angels who in heaven resides
We come before you,
Asking for your help in all things that we do.
We ask for your holy protection always,
At all times and in all situations,
So that the work we are meant to do in this world
Will not be disrupted or delayed in any way,
But will proceed with ease, peace, and blessings.
We call for round-the-clock protection,
We call for solid protection around our loved ones at all times, as well.
Keep us always in the brightest Light.
Keep us immune to the negative pulls

Of the world, people, or spirits.
Keep us happy and seeing the truth in every situation,
And free of judgments against our brethren.
Keep us always alert to potential dangers
Coming from any source whatsoever,
Whether seen or unseen, known or unknown.
And may we always have an avenue
Of escape from danger or mishap whenever necessary.
Let us truly be instruments of the Divine,
Seeing clearly what would be
The best course of action to take, if any,
In every situation before us.
Speak words of wisdom and counsel into our listening ears,
And see to it that we are always surrounded
By angels of light, protection, wisdom and love.
Let us truly reflect the presence of God on Earth as it is in Heaven.
Thank You God and Mother Mary and your Heavenly Host of Angels on High.

Pray for Peace

When the forces of darkness are battling
The light and the higher way,
Then it's time to call upon the power of love
That is a choice for us to use each day.

Love is the only solution,
And with it forgiveness can be;
For love is the true resolution
That will finally set you free.

Friend of the One Great Spirit,
Brothers and sisters of the light,
The time has come to pray for peace,
We need to work together to set the world right.

Pray for peace for the world is weary,
And there is far too much hatred at work here.
Pray for peace, it's the only solution
To bring an end to the killing and fear.

Pray for peace from that place inside you
And ask for Good Will to come,
With everyone's cooperation
There has to be some understanding found.

When there are those who hold the power
To wish to do great harm,
We have to realize only death and destruction comes
From those who wish to fight with arms.

War is not the answer,
It has never been and will never be;
We need to find a way to end the conflict,
We need to pray for peace.

May a little more love come into all hearts,
May a little more understanding be found,
May Good Will be our tool and intention
So we can find a way for love's higher ground.

Pray for peace, brothers and sisters
For in truth we are all one,
And when we find that peace within
We can share it with love 'til our work is done.

Lord Grant Me Strength

Lord, grant me the strength to overcome the binds of negativity and illusion
And any thoughts and judgments that limit myself or others.
Allow me to see the pure light of love that is within each of us,
Let the power of positive energy guide me and direct me
So that I can overcome the challenge that I encounter in life,
And find a way to choose to use
The gift of compassion and forgiveness in every difficult decision.

May I help others to also live from the light and love with your understanding,
May I remember and know that goodness and love will redeem us with God's love.
May love prevail so that I may be a servant of the light and a messenger of divine love,
May I share that love and light that is your presence so I may love more
To honor and see that presence in all.

Thank-You, God.

Prayers Sent by Heaven

There are these Prayers sent by Heaven
And the angels who watch over you
With light that will heal
And give you the strength you need to renew

The prayers sent by heaven
Are there to receive,
With blessings so true
If you can just be open and believe.

So be still beloved,
And take a few deep breaths,
And let the blessings of heaven be
So you can share them with those in need.

These messages that come
On the wings of a dove,
Are there to inspire you
With the Mother's great love.

Let that love light guide you
And all that you do,
And bring you comfort
That will always get you through.

For Spirit speaks in so many ways
And you know this is true,
That is why we connect everyday.

There are lessons and guidance
There waiting for you,
So don't hold back or stop what you do,
Have faith and allow the energy to continue.

There are prayers sent by heaven,
So open up to your soul and receive
The blessings that are waiting there
And Spirit will talk in so many ways to you.

And Mary Said Pray for Me

I heard a request from the Queen of Heaven that said
"Would you pray for me?"
And it resonated deep in my mind, so I asked
"Is this true?"
And I asked
"What would you have me pray for?"
"And how could my humble prayers make any difference?"
And I heard,

"Pray for all of the Servants of God
To find the strength to be able to do what they need to do,
And be aided in their work to be renewed.

Pray for the Angels, who constantly
Watch out for legions on the earthly plane.
Pray for my Love to be activated
So that it may be the guiding force of those
Who seek the Way on earth.

For there is so much need
For Kindness and Compassion.
There is such great need for Understanding
Of God's Plan for humanity.

And within each atom, within the Presence of Being
Within each ray of Light the prayers are heard.
The prayers change your vibration
And open the Channels to God's Heart.

And as you pray for Me,
You will be aligned
With the Light of God's Spirit.
And you will understand how I,
And how the ones of heaven and the Masters, pray.

So pray for me each day,
And for the Way to be clear
For what must be done for Good Will to succeed,

So Light and Love can fulfill God's Plan
So peace may prevail,
And Heaven may be known on earth here.

Make a Wish For The World

Make a wish for the World
As we all join together and pray
For the way to help humankind

Make a wish and remember we're all here to Join
In some way that we help to redeem the plan.
Each soul has a purpose
That resonates to why we are here
And how we all do what we can.

If you believe and you see
The way you can help
Your wishes will blossom
Like the garden in heaven
Each flower a gift to hold in your hands.

Make a wish for the world
And believe for a moment
We can make a difference
As we each join in spirit as one

Make a wish for the world
And when your time here is over
You might realize the seeds that you planted
Are blessings you left here

For there is still so much work to be done
Until we find that we are one,
There's a call to carry on each day
And such a never-ending need to pray.

For each who searches to find the way.
Make a wish and Believe
There is a better world that can be made
In the groundwork we lay

And do please remember
That prayers are answered every day

Beloved Mary, Queen of Angels Prayer

Beloved Mary Queen of Angels
You who hold open heavens space
Help me to have compassion
And forgiveness to heal the past
And bring me to your holy Grace

Mary Holy Mother, I call upon your energy
I ask you bring the Holy Spirit
To be alive inside of me

Let me share the breath of your being
To live within the heart of God's great love
I dedicate my path to the purpose
That you have shown for me to know

With your tender understanding
You open up the door
To the chosen one
And deliver me to the Lord

Let me be anointed
By the holy waters from the source
Let it quench my thirst for the beloved One
So I may serve as you would on Earth

Be my guide and teacher
Let me honor the Light of your Golden Orb
For the world's in needs of your mercy
Let my love help to bring it forth

Bring the crown of stars you wear
Down to circle me
Let me wear you're holy robe
So I can be surrounded with protection
To fulfill my destiny.

Let me breathe that holy spirit
Of the living light
So I may be with God in the service
As a disciple in my life

Allow the grace of your being
To transform my old mistaken ways
Let your inspiration guide me to you
When I'm lost and know not what to do

Holy mother full of Grace
Remove the binds of egos ties
Unchain the limitations
And Free me from the lies

Embrace me with your love
May is see your face in others I pray
let your life be an example
That inspires me ever day

Speak with whispers to my soul
Let your precious words be shown
To place upon life's altar
So I can offer them for others to know

Thank you Holy Mother
for your patience and your grace
Thank you Holy Spirit
For your presence that leads the way
And guides me with patience and understanding every day

Let your Love Guide Me

Lord, Let your love Guide me
In whatever comes my way.
May I be guided by the Highest good
This I now do pray.

Lord I ask that your energy be with me
As I do my work today
And may I speak with kindness

And let compassion purpose lead my way.

Let your love bring forth blessings
In what I do and say
And may there be some understanding
That there are Miracles at work each day.

For within the billions particles
That are in every atom here
There is the holy energy
That with God's Love can appear.

Let me see beyond the form
Let the greater picture now appear,
So I may be free of the drama life brings
And your light can shine and the path made clear.

Lord let your love be my anchor,
And your light shine my way
And let your guidance bring forth blessings,
So that I may serve with love today.

Lord Light the Fire of My Soul

Lord, light the fire of my soul
To burn with your pure Spirit so I may know
The gift of your presence and amazing Grace
That leads me to see the path to your Holy space

Lord, Let me experience your forgiveness
And the great gift of compassion to be
Able to reveal what I hide in me
That shows up as faults in others I see.

May I learn from this forgiveness
And the mercy that you show
For all of God's lost children that are blinded
By the direction of the domain of the ego.

Lord light the fire of my spirit

So it may be a torch so Bright
To give me the Vision to know
How to fulfill the purpose of my soul

Let me share your teachings
That you so wisely bring
So that I learn from each day
From the challenges and joy in everything

Let me have a humble heart
So pride does divide me
From those lessons I can learn from
In this Dharma you impart

Lord burn away the veils of illusions
And the darkness of the world
So I can clearly see
the vision so Divine in everything

And Light the way to find the path to thee
With the blessings you bring
Be given back in service to those in need
So I may so your love reach all eventually

Lord Hear My Prayer

Lord hear my prayer
And may I be quiet enough to hear
The words you give to me
That let's me know your presence is near

For every word you offer
Is water for a thirsty heart
This very broken jar I offer
That needs your love to do my part

Lord hear my prayer
And let me be open to receive
The answers and solutions
That I know will be there for me

May I have the courage
To follow the guidance that you give
May I be a faithful servant
Of the way you'd have me live

And when I walk in darkness
Let your light show me how
To understand and have courage
To fulfill my souls true call

Let me accept what is
And whatever I must do
So I may learn the lessons I need
So may better serve you

Lord let me hear your prayers
And I wonder who you pray to
Is it us and all the weary souls
That so need your help
So we can evolve and grow

Into the reflection of heaven
To fulfill our lives with your love
And become we were created to be
With kindness and love we show

I thank you lord and the masters
And Mother Mary too
When we are in need you are there
We always can talk to you

Lord Let Me Be a Force For Good

Lord, let me be a force for good,
Trusting where you lead me to be;
Let the grace of God's true love
Be the power that is alive in my true energy.

Let me be of service, Lord,
And help me to have a strong foundation here.
Let your light come though me

And be used for others in the best way I can share.

Let there be a perfect balance
And let the heart speak to my mind.
To allow your words find their purpose
In ways that I might not ever find.

Let Peace be my core of being,
And Love as my teacher while I am here.
With a Light that shines right through me
And eliminates any fear that may be there.

And may the perfect presence
Of spirit come through me
And let that spirit guide me
And show me the way when I can't see.

And when the burdens get heavy,
Please lift the load and carry me
To the place where I can find
The strength of Peace inside to be.

So I can be of service
With Joy as my keynote,
And release all of the worries
So I can be a servant of your love.

A Prayer to Life

We build cathedrals as a way to show our love to God.
We build temples to the visions that show us the way
So we can live and worship with the power that comes
From those who are here to pray each day.

And the breath of spirit comes to us
And this spirit is free to be
A prayer to life, and the inspiration of the heart
And the truth that can set us free.

And every prayer and candle lit
And every breath that feeds our souls
Is strengthened by the believing,
For as we believe in our hearts it is so.

We are the living the light of Being
Here in this time and place,
And sometimes the secrets we need
Are buried so deep it takes a lifetime to be revealed.

The One, the whole, the individual
Are all bonded in God's energy,
And as we save our soul while we're here
This is somehow the salvation for all who care.

And we see the precious jewels of love
That shine with the magic of such Bright Light
And we place the crown of creation
On the ones who are willing to carry it through the night.

And we believe in our true purpose,
And the ones who hold the plan.
And we offer our prayers to the presence
Of peace throughout the land.

And we believe in truth,
And we hope and pray the truth will set us free.
And we believe in love and ask with our hearts
That purpose in our lives will let that love be.

Dear Lord

Dear Lord,
If I were to open the doors of Perception,
Would my heart hear the song of the universe
As it celebrated your love?

Would the music of the spheres lift me up
To meet your spirit and free me
'Til the echoes of your energy reverberated through my soul

To hear the calling of the one voice
That resides in the Holy Word?

And would I strive to express
The inexpressible truth that resides in Your Being?
If not how can I in my silence reflect you
And all the glory you bring to me?

Is your secret my treasure to honor,
Or is it a key to share with all who are here
On the path to discover our true destination
Which is our eternal promise
To become one with this magnet of energy from the source?

And I would hold your love in my heart
As a jewel to shine with the light of a thousand suns.
And I would cherish your presence in my soul
As a marriage that is joined
In the gift of your being alive.

As a silent partner who embraces me
With the gift of eternal love.
And I would let your hymn of praise be my
Mantra , my anthem, and my purpose

And so I thank you, and as you show me the way;
I listen in the silence to hear the calling of your voice
To awaken me from my illusory dreams and
Guide me on the journey home.

Lord and Mother of The Light

Lord and Mother of the Light,
Lead me to believe so that I might see
The opening of Spirit awaiting me,
In the radiant beauty in Heaven's fields.

There are fields of Gold and fields of Green
All shining in their own astral dreams,
Fields of Promise from the past
Let my spirit be free to be there at last.

And when my body is ready to be done,
And the earth and it's lessons can be viewed from the soul,
May I be able to release the hold this earth has had
And see the opening that now appears
And what awaits with my journey there.

Let the Angels be here with me
For the Guardians at the Gate await at the opening,
And there is a great light that shines forth the Way
To a new a brighter place to stay.

And with the grace of awakening
There is such a gratitude felt that can set us free,
And when the time comes to say farewell
And fly with wings of angels on high.

To a new beginning in a brighter light,
To the realms of heaven
That await my sight,
To the fields of Glory lit by the Mother's eyes.

Lord, let your love guide me
In whatever comes my way,
May I be guided by the Highest Good
This I now do pray.

The Miracles The Mother Brings

Can you see the Miracles the Mother brings
That Blesses you when you pray
Can you embody the Holy Spirit
That brings these gifts your way

Can you really feel
The good that God does bring
With the presence of the Holy Mother
And her compassion that holds us in Presence of her being

You are part of this one great Light
You are part of the holy heart
That holds us all in such a loving space
As you find our way through the illusion of this earthly place

Can you see the Beauty
Of the light surrounding you
And the grace that comes and blesses you
That is forever is there to help and to renew

Can you really see the way
That she sees deep into your heart
To help you to fulfill your part

She saves you with the smile she brings
For there is such a purity
And there is this heavenly glow
That she blesses you to know

If you can just love yourself enough
To forgive the mistakes you've made
And then really feel the depths of compassion
And the power to live with the love it takes

So ask for the amazing grace
To embrace you and hold you tight
And bring the blessings of the Mothers love
So that you can be healed and make things right

Find a way to believe
That you can make a brand new start
You can be living with the blessings
Of the love that she brings into your heart.

See the Miracles that Mary brings
To transform your life with a just a prayer
We say Thank You to God
For the Holy Birth that lives forever more

Lord Let Me See Beyond the Form

Lord I ask that your energy be with me
As I do my work today
And may I speak with kindness
And let compassion purpose lead my way.

Let your love bring forth blessings
In what I do and say
And may there be some understanding
That there are Miracles at work each day.

For within the billions particles
That are in every atom here
There is the holy energy
That with God's Love can appear.

Let me see beyond the form
Let the greater picture now appear,
So I may be free of the drama life brings
And your light can shine and the path made clear.

Lord let your love be my anchor,
And your light shine my way
And let your guidance bring forth blessings,
So that I may serve with love today

A Prayer for Guidance

Lord when I pray
And hear not the answers
To what I think really matters
Let me have faith in the masters

So I can receive their guidance
And when I go into the silence
Let the strength be given
And your Holy light to find it

Allow me to see the signs you send
In such mysterious ways my precious friend
So I may smile and know

That you will guide on the way to go

And when confusion and doubt descend
And darkness blocks my vision
Let my apprehension be forgiven
So may continue on the path you've given

For I wish to serve the plan
And continue as disciple if I can
And when love is hidden from me
Allow me the grace to still believe

That there is a purpose I am here for
And blessings come eventually
So I learn that life shows us many solutions
And the lessons I learn will produce them

To find better way to choose
The path that I need to best serve you
To live with your love and be free
'Til heaven on earth can be seen

And lord so I pray
And that we all can learn a better way to live
Grant us compassion and the grace to forgive
'Til way can find a way
To live in peace one day

A Prayer for Good Will in The World

Lord, let the Pure Energy of Good Will,
Bring the power of Right Actions into the world.
May every willing heart choose to act in a way
That's aligned with Love and Light.

May confidence in the destiny of the people who play a role in the aid of the world bring
Right Actions into us.

We pray for the world,
We Pray for peace,
We pray for growth in the most positive way.

And may all of the ones who have a way to help,
Help in every way they may.

As the world works together
For the good of the people of the world,
We are a united force that can bring
This precious planet and it's people
Into harmony, yes harmony,
Into a united force for good,
Where all can benefit and be filled with
Light and the blessings of love.
Working with wisdom and serving God's Will
With Good Will for all,
Always holding Good Will for all.

The Rewards

As I approached the end of the writing of this book I got this message that was a little different from the others. I felt that that these teachings are part of work that we can share with the world to now to help bring in new balancing energy to the world. That as we actually become these teachings and we will embody the energy of the Mother here on Earth. This will do great service as we embody the Love and grace of her energy on earth. I keep receiving the message that we are to merge as one with this Divine energy so we can be able to hold the torch of her loving light.

These are the last of the messages I received for this book, however I do feel their will be more coming for a future book

I feel so humbled and honored to be able to participate in this process that is unfolding with the Grace of God. I thank each of you for having an open heart and mind and participating in the spirit that blesses us and the world as we continue to serve Father Mother God's purpose and plan to bring heaven to earth and more loving kindness to humankind.

The Torch

And now we are given the torch to bear,
And now we hold the holy chalice divine.

And we say "Yes" to the path that opens
To behold a new awakening to a higher light.

For so long we have been seeking
And we have asked to be shown the way,
To be disciples in the making
And now we realize the new awakening.

And now the light is given,
And now the life is shown,
And we embrace the initiation
And the rebirth in our souls.

And we become the ones,
Who offer up our hearts,
To find there is a place inside us
For us to make a brand new start.

The path moves ever onward,
And spiral up to a brilliant light,
And heaven's bridge is now reaches
The spirit in our heart of hearts.

And there are now legions
Of Angels who guide the way,
To the ones who are agents who know
The path of those Masters enlightened souls.

And we light the path,
And we show the way,
To help others to find their true purpose
And together we do pray.

And we merge and hold the energy,
And we bring the power of light to see,
That we are the love of the creator
We are so blessed and thankful to serve this divine energy.

You Are a Fragile Petal

You are a fragile petal that falls from the Mother's garden in heaven
That carries the fragrance of the exquisite beauty of creations.

You hold the keys to the kingdom,
You hold the wisdom of the ages,
You are the gift of God's making.

It is time to celebrate who you really are,
A beloved reflection of the Mother love
Alive right here in this time and space
To behold the gift of this Amazing Grace.

Celebrate the ascension and unification
Of the Mother into her new place
Bringing a balance to the human race.

Celebrate the blessings that come
As we all reflect this gift of being
Alive here and now merged as one
With the love of creation,
The unification of Father Mother God
And man merged as one.

Healing Prayer

Mother Mary I do pray,
For your blessed Presence to be with me
As I walk on the path
And seek to live with your love each day.

To help me do whatever it takes
To heal my life,
Make things right
With the power of God's redeeming light.

So with compassion I might find
That heavenly grace
That brings redemption to save,
And the love that opens up the way.

To find the understanding that lives
To help us get past the separation
And ego that divides the world
From the purpose of peace we came for.

Give us the power to believe
That with your loving Presence,
We can all do our part to heal
All the broken lives eventually.

And I pray for all those who seek relief,
All those suffering and in need,
May Heaven's Light shine bright
And bless us with your love divine.

Mother Mary I do bow in awe
At the Miracles that you bring,
I thank you for your gifts combined
With the love of Christ's Great Blessed Light.

Sending you my deep love and Blessings of love always
Rev. Dr. Cindy Paulos

If you wish to stay in touch you can find more daily messages on my
website. cindypaulos.com
http://www.marysmessagesoflove.com/
https://www.facebook.com/revCindyPaulos/

So many miracles have happened,
So much love God's given me,
So many blessings have been seen
And I'm grateful for everything.

And now enough has been spoken,
And now enough has been said,
It's time to release it all to God
And let spirit guide the way ahead.

Epilogue

"Blessed is she who believed that what was spoken to her by the Lord would be fulfilled" (Lk1:45)

The process of connecting with Mary has truly changed my life. After about two years since the first contact with Her, I completed the book you are now reading. I felt as if I have made a very deep connection in this miraculous relationship with Mary.

I had not realized I had some very deep wounds that were related to abuse that needed healing. With her loving guidance I found healing and I also was able to see into what had kept me from having a deeper connection to Jesus Christ.

I had always sensed that I had been subjected to torture and had been burned at the stake in a previous life by some who did not like my views in the Catholic Church. I have seen many lifetimes that I had experienced when I was in my teens after my enlightenment experience. This particular lifetime had left me very angry and cynical about religion and what has been done in the name of Christ. I did not stop me from reaching out to Him in a direct mystical way.

During the final stages of writing this book there some very deep healing that occurred with Mary's help. What I was surprised by, was a very strong message from Mary that I was now being delivered to Christ to continue my healing and growth. I have to admit I was a little sad and did not feel as if I was quite ready to leave her loving energy and support yet. She assured me this was a very great honour and a good thing. She assured me she would still be there when I called upon her and needed her presence.

I am very happy to say that has proven to be true. She still has Her presence available to call upon. I am now reaching out to Jesus Christ and developing a closer relationship with him. There is a different energy vibration that is so transcendent with His grace and love.

I am still getting messages from Mary to create another journal, Spoken Word CD and calendar. These are already in the works. However I am also being directing by Christ and have been able to drop feeling like a martyr and victim. With some of the principles Mary shared with me and I shared with you in this book, I was able to forgive, release and understand the bigger picture.

I am so deeply grateful for these life changing gifts given to me by Mary and I hope that by sharing them you may also find a loving relationship and friend in Her and Jesus Christ.

Sometimes the last words are the hardest,
Maybe there is always so much more to say.
And if I just write a little more
Perhaps I'll get it right today.

For all those words that were never spoken
And all those things that were never said,
For all the music never written
From the songs there in my head.

I offer all this to spirit
To take and to release,
To scatter to the four directions
A prayer now to be freed.

So many miracles have happened,
So much love God's given me,
So many blessings have been seen,
And I'm so grateful for everything.

And now enough has been spoken,
And now enough has been said,
It's time to release it all to God
And let spirit guide the way ahead.

Mary's Blessings

May you dance with angels,
May they lead your way
To see the beauty of life
That surrounds you each day.

May the holy dove
Sing to your heart with love
To comfort you with wings
That enfold you with love.

May the radiance of heaven
Shine forth its light upon you,
And the one true source
Lift you up when your blue.

May you find the answers
To the questions you seek,
May the truth provide you
With the understanding you need.

May the music of the heavenly spheres
Sing to your soul
And embrace you with the majesty
And the glory to know.

There is a higher power
That is always present and can be
Alive in your life
Whenever you're in need.

May kindness and patience
Always find a way
To help to change your life,
For you to find more compassion today.

Thank-you God and the Holy Mother too,
Thanks to the Angels for all they do,
May the blessings of God's love
Always be alive in you.

The image above was created by my granddaughter Haley Alvarado.

Mother Mary has many faces. She appears in a myriad of ways.
The images in this book were created by myself and were inspired by a
variety of classical images.
I am not an artist but I do see visions and I tried to share images that spoke
to me.
The graphic presentations were created with patience by Dr. Michael Likey.
Thank you to Paul Sandefur for the artwork on plate 8's Forgiveness
chapter.
I believe that the Spirit of Mary goes beyond any image I might try to use to
convey her Divine Presence.
These images will be available in color cards for the holidays.
To see daily images and words go to <u>MysticalMotherMary.com</u>

Deep Gratitude

This book could not be made possible without the help and support of many angelic beings. I was touched by the wonderful help of a Mother Mary team that stepped up to the plate to give loving insight.

My heart had been deeply touched by the devotion of Dr. Michael Likey who edited the book and worked with me on creating the cover art. His devotion was a constant inspiration and the book would not have been possible without his help. Rev. Mary Omwake, and Bob Miles were part of the inner core team that inspired me along the way.

Thanks to my friends Bob Stone, Paula Sandefur for her contribution, Michelle Behr, Andrea and Gary Smith, Delmary, Jessie Close, Claire Papin, Judie Stein, Warren and Denise Eckstein, and Dyan Garris. Love to Kenya and Oscar Autie and my inspired Grammy friends. A special thank you to John Detz, who has been a wonderful lifetime companion and for so long in this life. To all my radio friends at KAOI RADIO GROUP.

Special thanks and love to my family—to my beautiful daughter, Heather Paulos, my awesome grandchildren, Max and Haley, my sisters Pamela, Jennifer, and Charmaine, Marlene Dlouhy, and nieces Dawn Kawamura and Francesca Gamboa.

Thanks to all my social media friends and supporters. I appreciate your support and likes!

While writing this book my step-father, friend and mentor Dr. Paul Masters and my friend Dr. Wayne Dyer made their transitions. I have felt their presence often while writing these words and I thank their Spirit and presence for such loving light and guidance. And thanks to all the ones I love who have passed to the other side but still whisper in my ear.

My deepest gratitude goes to God, Christ, Mother Mary and all the Teachers, the Masters, the Beloved Angels and all the silent ones who watch and guide us on our way.

-Rev. Dr. Cindy Paulos
June 2016

About The Author

Cindy Paulos is a minister, writer, speaker, teacher, artist, composer, lyricist, videographer, and travel agent, as well as an award-winning radio and TV personality.

Cindy has been writing inspired poetry and words of wisdom for most of her life. She began her spiritual connection at the age of 12, which expanded into a profound experience of light at age 15. Since then, she has received inspiration and guidance from her spiritual source through messages and song.

Rev. Paulos received her ministerial credentials at the age of 17 from the University of Metaphysics in Los Angeles where she became the youngest instructor to ever teach there. Dr. Paulos has been teaching meditation and how to connect with God ever since. In 1978 she received her Doctor of Metaphysical Science degree.

She owned her own music store, Paulos Music, in Westwood, Los Angeles, at the age of 18. She worked as a DJ at the world-famous KROQ in Los Angeles, then moved to Northern California and started KVRE Radio and worked as the Program Director and morning person for 8 years. In 1989 she moved to Maui and co-founded KAOI RADIO GROUP. Dr. Paulos hosts the longest-running talk show on Maui, interviewing celebrities, political leaders, and spiritual teachers. She also is a DJ on KAOI FM. She hosted a local TV music show, "Local Licks," for 5 years, interviewing many local music stars.

She started a non-profit organization called Metaphysical Media

Network and a 24/7 spiritual internet radio station in 2015 and has many shows on a spiritual nature on Blog Talk Radio.

Cindy's first book, *Put a Little Light in your Life: a Guide to Sending and Receiving Positive Energy*, is available in hard and soft cover and as an e-book. Her second book is about stress-free travel and is called *The Travel Angel Handbook*. An accomplished composer who was inspired by the transition of her mother, Paulos produced and recorded an album of original songs, *There Is a Forever*. (For more information, go to BrightLightMusic.com.) She has also composed and recorded a CD of songs about Maui called, *Practicing Aloha*, which received the Hawaii Music Award in the inspirational category. She became a voting member of the National Academy of Recording Artist, (Grammys) that year. She released her third book, *Angel Blessings, Messages from Heaven* in 2014 and also released a double CD called Angel Blessings, Benefitting Hospice that year. In 2015 she released her fourth CD, *Arise above Abuse*.

Cindy is a travel agent and has co-hosted a travel show on KAOI AM for years. She has traveled extensively throughout the world, visiting Egypt, China, Greece, Japan, France, Spain, England, Thailand, Nepal, Tibet and many other countries.

Cindy's book and CD's are available at cindypaulos.com.

Rev. Dr. Cindy Paulos

PO BOX 84
Wailuku HI 96793

cindypaulos.com
http://www.marysmessagesoflove.com/
https://www.facebook.com/revCindyPaulos/

Other Works by Rev. Cindy Paulos
Books
Put a Little Light in Your Life, A Guide for Sending and Receiving Positive Energy

The Travel Angel Handbook

Angel Blessings, Messages from Heaven

CD'S
There is a Forever

Practicing Aloha

Angel Blessings Benefitting Hospice

Arise Above Abuse

All available at cindypaulos.com

http://www.marysmessagesoflove.com/

https://www.facebook.com/revCindyPaulos/

Made in the USA
San Bernardino, CA
07 July 2016